מסורה

ArtScroll Series™

Rabbi Nosson Scherman / Rabbi Meir Zlotowitz

General Editors

Anatomy

by
Akiva Tatz

with a Foreword by
Joseph Tanenbaum

# of a Search

Personal Drama in the Teshuva Revolution

Published by

Mesorah Publications, ltd.

FIRST EDITION
First Impression ... April, 1987
Second Impression ... July, 1998
Third Impression ... October, 2001
Fourth Impression ... July 2006
Fifth Impression ... April 2013
Sixth Impression ... August 2018
Seventh Impression ... May 2022

Published and Distributed by
MESORAH PUBLICATIONS, Ltd.
313 Regina Avenue / Rahway, New Jersey 07065

Distributed in Europe by
LEHMANNS
Unit E, Viking Business Park
Rolling Mill Road
Jarrow, Tyne & Wear NE32 3DP
England

Distributed in Australia & New Zealand by
GOLDS WORLD OF JUDAICA
3-13 William Street
Balaclava, Melbourne 3183
Victoria Australia

Distributed in Israel by
SIFRIATI / A. GITLER — BOOKS
POB 2351
Bnei Brak 51122

Distributed in South Africa by
KOLLEL BOOKSHOP
Northfield Centre, 17 Northfield Avenue
Glenhazel 2192, Johannesburg, South Africa

THE ARTSCROLL® SERIES
ANATOMY OF A SEARCH
© Copyright 1987, by MESORAH PUBLICATIONS, Ltd.
313 Regina Avenue / Rahway, N.J. 07065 / (718) 921-9000 / www.artscroll.com

ISBN 10: 0-89906-550-3 / ISBN 13: 978-0-89906-550-2
ITEM CODE: ANAH

Cover design by Ben Gasner, Jerusalem

Typography by Compuscribe at ArtScroll Studios, Ltd.
Bound by Sefercraft, Quality Bookbinders, Ltd. Rahway, NJ

For my parents שיח׳

whose greatness

is beyond description.

מרדכי ניפטער
ישיבת טלז
RABBI MORDECAI GIFTER
28570 NUTWOOD LANE
WICKLIFFE, OHIO 44092

בע״ה — ר״ח ניסן, תשמ״ז

עלי ההגהה של ספרו האנגלי של דר. עקיבא טאטץ, נר״ו, הגיעוני.
ולעונג הוא לראות שניץ ונכד ממשפחת הגאון ר׳ מאיר אטלס ז״ל,
אב״ד שאול במדינת ליטא — ואחד מחבורת שלשת האברכים גדולי
תורה בטלז שקבעו אבני יסוד לישיבת עץ חיים, ישיבת טלז — נתעורר
לשוב לשרשיו.

בטח יפעלו דבריו על אלה המכירים בריקנות חיים ללא תורה ומצוה.
אכן עיקר הכל לא בויכוחים בעניני אמונה, ליישב קושיות באמונה. אלא
בלימוד התוה״ק כהלכתה, שאז אין המסתפק מוצא תירוצים לקושיותיו
אלא שחש ומרגיש שאין כאן לא קושיא ולא ספק, ומתקיים בו ,,באורך
נראה אור״׳

יזכה המחבר היקר נר״ו, לקרב רחוקים ללימוד התוה״ק ולהגיע לידי
קיום רצונו יתברך באמת ולב תמים.

מנאי, אוהב נאמן לכל אוהבי תורת ה׳,

[signature]

Letter from HaGaon Rabbi Mordechai Gifter, שליט״א, Rosh Yeshiva of the Telshe Yeshiva,
Wickliffe, Ohio.

RABBI S. WASSERMAN
PONIM MEIROT 15/10
MATERSDORF, JERUSALEM
ISRAEL (02) 537-420

הרב שמחה וסרמן
רח פנים מאירות 15/10
מטרסדורף - ירושלים

בס"ד ירושלים עיה"ק ת"ו ,   ד' אדר תשמ"ז

מחבר הספר ש"ב הרב דר. עקיבא סאץ הי"ו הוא נין ונכד גדולי ומאורי תוה"ק
ממשפחת אסלס-מארגענשטסערן . משפחה זו שמעה פסירת אא"ז מו"ר הגאון ר' מאיר
אסלס זצ"ל ממיסדי ישיבת סעלז ופסירת הגאון הר' משה ברוך מארגענשטערן זצ"ל
הי' נראה כאילו ח"ו נס ליחה וכיההה קינה במדינת אפריקה הדרומית, נתקיימו
בה דברי חז"ל ב"מ פ"ה א"ר פרנך אר"י כל שהוא ח"ח ובנו ח"ח ובן בנו ח"ח
שוב אין תורה פוסקת מזרעו לעולם, דייקו לומר, שאעפ"י שפעמים פוסקת מ"מ
אין ההפסק לעולם ושוב שבה תוה"ק לאכסנייתה, שבה המשפחה להציץ ציץ ולהוציא
פרח ע"י המחבר שזכה לעזוב את הבקר וירץ אחרי אליהו (מלכים א' י"ט ס-כ) ללון
בעומקה של הלכה בכולל משך חכמה אור יהושע שע"י ישיבת אור שמח פעיה"ק ת"ו .
יה"ר שיזכה בחיבורו זה לאהב את המקום על הבריות ולקרב לבות אחב"י לאביהם
שבשמים ולקרב מלכות שמים כמ"ש לאאע"ה והי' ברכה ופירש"י בן חנמין שסיום
וחתימה הגלות תהי' ע"י ירושת אאע"ה בקירוב לבות הבריות לאביהם שבשמים
כנפשו ונפש ש"ב מכבדו

אלעזר שמחה וסרמן

Letter from HaGaon Rabbi Elazar Simcha Wasserman, שליט"א, Rosh Yeshiva of Yeshivas
Ohr Elchonon, Jerusalem, son of HaGaon Rabbi Elchonon Wasserman, זצ"ל היי"ד.

Foreword

When my parents, Avraham and Chippa Sarah Tanenbaum, arrived at Halifax, Newfoundland in 1916, they brought with them their traditions and loyalties. But they also felt the immediate pressure and need to provide security and a future for their children. Though most of that generation maintained a love for and pride in their Judaism, they were, in a sense, too burdened with *parnassa* problems to set up proper Jewish educational systems for the next generation. Thank G-d, some efforts were made, and that is why our communities did survive.

But for the most part, youngsters received poor training and little inspiration. Those were tough times. Eking out a living took most of the juice out of you.

And so it was no wonder that so many of the next generation, and of course the succeeding one, drifted further and further away from our sources and heritage. But somehow the strength and love of Torah has never left our people completely. And even a small number holding on has been sufficient to bridge the gap. (Maybe it is symbolic that one of my businesses was building bridges.) And now we see traffic coming across that bridge in the other direction. Thousands of young people who received no Jewish education are today, in their adult years, searching out and reconnecting themselves with their Judaism.

That's what this book is all about. For myself, as someone who has observed, anticipated and participated in these ups-and-downs, I take great pleasure in recommending these stories which describe a new "up."

Dr. Akiva Tatz's book begins in Johannesburg, but it could have been, and in fact for many was, Toronto, New York and London. It's the story of a generation who fooled the pessimists and justified our faith in our people's power of renewal.

Contents

This edition is in tribute to

Mr. and Mrs. Ervin Landau

in recognition of their leadership in the

Teshuva Revolution

בס"ד

Acknowledgments

Nothing in this book is original except its shortcomings. Sources other than those quoted directly in the text are Rabbi Moshe Shapira, Rabbi Moshe Shirken, Rabbi Avigdor Miller, Rabbi Yisroel Aryeh Shulman and Rabbi Avraham Hassan.

Rabbi Simcha Wasserman says that *teshuva* is in the air now, inflammable; one has only to strike a light and it flames up. To my friends in the yeshiva, especially those whose stories are told here (names and details have been changed), may your stories help bring others closer to Hashem ית' and His Torah.

I wish to thank:

• My Rabbonim and teachers in South Africa and Israel, far more than can be expressed here;

• Rabbi Nota Schiller and Rabbi Mendel Weinbach and their colleagues at Ohr Somayach for their daring vision that late starters in Torah learning could make it to the top, and for the teaching and inspiration they personally provide in making this happen;

• Rabbi Yehoshua Bezalel Kaplan for making this book possible in addition to all his unsung deeds;

• Rabbi Meir Zlotowitz, Rabbi Nosson Scherman, Rabbi Sheah Brander of ArtScroll/Mesorah Publications for adding a new dimension to Torah literature — it is a privilege to be associated with them;

• Rabbi Avie Gold for his meticulous concern and efficiency in honing the book in its final stages;

• Reb Shmuel Blitz, Reb Eli Kroen, Mrs. Faygie Weinbaum, Mrs. Simie Korn and Menuchah Marcus of the ArtScroll team for their efficient handling of all the details, technical and editorial, in the production of this book;

• Joseph and Galia Berry for unlimited help over the past few months;

• Mrs. Chava Pearl for her expert typing of the manuscript;

• My wife Suzanne שתחי' more than anyone. May Hashem יח' grant us both the זכות to continue giving some of what we have received.

And to "Meshech Chochma Ohr Yehoshua," the unique kollel with a reputation as the most intensive in Israel, where newcomers to Torah only a few short years ago learn side by side with people who have been living Torah from birth and learning it from the time they began to speak, and to the great man who heads it, these stories are a tribute to you.

A.T.
Adar 5747
March 1987

Preface

One day some months ago, just before afternoon *seder* in the kollel was due to begin, I happened to be in one of the yeshiva's dormitory rooms. Some newcomers to Ohr Somayach were sitting around exchanging tales of the events and circumstances that had brought them there, and singing — someone had an old guitar and they were singing songs of the last few years, reminiscing.

"There's a light,
A certain kind of light,
That never shone on me ..."

I was struck by the music and the faces and the stories, and I found myself re-living my own recent past. Each one had an amazing tale to tell, of thirsting, searching, and of a road that had led him to Torah, and I decided then to tell the stories of the people in that room and of some of those who have crossed paths with them over the past few months here in Jerusalem.

The music followed me down the stairs on my way back to the *beis midrash*...

"Knock, knock, knockin' on Heaven's door ..."

---

seder: learning session
kollel: advanced section of yeshiva for married students
beis midrash: study hall

Body and Soul

CAUSE UNKNOWN

The first thing I saw at medical school was a dead man. From that first day in the anatomy dissection hall as I peeled back the heavy sheet from the cadaver I was to dissect, everything seemed different. I had begun to wonder about purpose and meaning, and delving into that human body daily, discovering its wonders and simultaneously facing death, exposed a vague emptiness; he seemed to be challenging me, demanding that I examine myself and define where I was going. He had been a young man; the label on the sheet said: "Cause of death unknown"; and in a way he was me. Even the best medical school teaches only sophisticated plumbing, really, and does not answer the existential questions; if anything it raises them, presents paradoxes: man is an accidental creature distantly descended from an ameba and closely related to an ape, and yet his life is worth saving. It did not make sense.

I had never thought much beyond myself until then: I had not been searching for anything in particular, and the question of ultimate meaning had never really bothered me, probably because my life in the day-to-day present had been so full. I had grown up in the lap of South African luxury and lacked nothing: money, servants who did everything from polishing shoes to serving breakfast in bed, weekends on the tennis court and by the pool, holidays on the Cape's breathtaking beaches or on safari in the national game parks, endless entertainment; in short, all the gracious ease that was South Africa. I owned three motorcycles before I was eighteen, and an Italian convertible. I spent a year in the United States on a student exchange scholarship and studied medicine. And far more important than all this were my friends, exceptional individuals attuned to much more than the usual concerns of youth. Our friendships were deep and lasting, our loyalty unshakable (and still is). I had everything I wanted and enjoyed it all.

Now life and death became real issues, and the drama of medical training magnified them. As an intern in a busy hospital I felt it more acutely; treatment decisions are made by the consultants but it is the intern who sits at the bedside late at night holding the hand of the dying. The stark drama of surgery too, made a deep impression — my surgical training was at hospitals in Johannesburg's Black and Colored townships, and the experience was unforgettable. At Baragwanath, Africa's largest hospital which serves Soweto's one million inhabitants, weekends are a constant stream of surgical emergencies, mostly the result of violence in the township. Interns suture huge wounds (anything less than a major wound is sutured by orderlies — the doctors could never cope with the load) in the surgical casualty department which is known as "the Pit." The scene resembles the aftermath of a battle and one is never quite sure how everyone gets treated. One weekend evening when one of the surgical chiefs of many years' experience — and who happens to be Jewish — was walking through the "Pit" on his way to the ward, a motionless patient on a stretcher caught his attention. He leaned over the man for a few moments and said quietly to his intern, "Pass me a knife." The surprised intern handed him a scalpel. Without ceremony he opened the patient's chest on the spot and repaired a stabbed heart. The man lived.

But the outcome was not always so good. On one occasion in another hospital after our surgical unit had been up all night in the operating theater battling for the life of a Colored street-gang leader who had multiple stab wounds inflicted by a rival gang, the word went out that the surgery had been successful and that it seemed he would live. That afternoon during visiting hours the enemy gang arrived for a "visit," gathered round his bed, and as nurses scattered and patients hid under their beds, they finished off the job with hatchets.

A secular background does not provide a meaningful framework for dealing with the issues raised by these experiences, and I found my sense of existential unease deepening. In my third year at medical school, studying pathology and microbiology and with little contact with living patients, I went through a mild crisis of identity and direction and began to wonder whether medicine was for me altogether, but could not see any clear alternative which offered the fulfillment I desired.

My close friends were experiencing similar ordeals and our generation in general was going through a nebulous, undefined period. The mood had always been brought closest to our consciousness in the music; we had always been close to the music, drenched in it, sure that somewhere on that album or the next the answers lay, and it had been the music which focused our emotions. Folk had given way to the protest music of the 'sixties, and we had been swept along with the anti-establishment anger, the fierce determination to return to integrity. Dylan had said it all, and they were days heady with an illusion of purpose. But the 'seventies had not brought an answer. Rock and roll was an inarticulate digression and as the decade progressed it became clear that the emptiness of Western society had been exposed for us but that no-one was offering any alternative. The music that had been haunting in its reach for a deliverance of youth became haunted. A disintegration began, a movement to many cults and a generalized escape into drugs; nothing seemed clear, and we were desperately in need of a point of definite contact with reality.

A MAN CALLED SHABBOS

On campus at that time a series of *shiurim* on medical *halacha* began, given by a Rabbi from the "Kollel" community, and later, on *Yiddishkeit* in general by a certain architect who has

---

shiur(im): lecture(s)   *halacha:* Torah law   *Yiddishkeit:* Judaism

probably inspired more *ba'alei teshuva* than anyone else in South Africa and quite possibly anywhere. He spoke about Torah and learning, the beauty of human relationships and marriage in the Torah framework, about personal development and purpose in life; and through his low-key, good-humored style I began to perceive clearly the dichotomy between the secular and the Torah worlds, the shifting sands of utilitarianism and the permissive slide towards non-values on the one hand, and the sublime elevation, the reaching far beyond the self and locking into an absolute dimension on the other. He spoke about *hachnasas orchim* and invited everyone for Shabbos. When I arrived for a Shabbos at his home I found twenty other people there too — he invites everyone at every *shiur* he gives and sometimes they all come. His wife never knows how many there will be and his children give their beds to guests week after week. In the Kollel community I found that everyone is like that, actions exceed words; all have guests and yet rush to invite any additional newcomers home from *shul* on Friday night. My friends at university who studied philosophy or the arts or even religion developed intellectually but not necessarily personally; people in the Torah world were doing nothing other than developing personally. Morals in the secular world were fluid and the campus resembled a zoo, whereas in the Torah community modesty and self-control were the values looked up to, and very soon it became obvious which road leads towards integrity in the deepest sense and where all other roads lead.

That Shabbos experience made a major impact on me. The first thing that struck me on Shabbos in that home was that no-one was going anywhere. The familiar rush of each member of the family to his own activities was absent, everyone was together and simply enjoying being there. I began to learn about Shabbos and discovered that it represents the dimension of essential existence as opposed to that of becoming; the weekdays are spent building, developing, constantly moving towards a goal, whereas Shabbos is itself something of that ultimate and absolute goal — *me'eyn olam*

---

ba'alei teshuva: those engaged in rediscovering Torah Judaism
hachnasas orchim: hospitality   *Shabbos:* the Sabbath   *shul:* synagogue

haba — a fractional representation of the world-to-come, that is, the state of permanent and true existence which transcends physicality infinitely. Translated into action, on Shabbos the individual and the family are not going anywhere; they have arrived. The experience is that of simply and actually *being*, and in this lies the secret of its bliss, the indescribable feeling of intrinsic existence, of permanence within mutability. The whole week attains meaning in the light of Shabbos, the process of becoming in itself taking on a dimension of the "having-become" when directed towards the focus of Shabbos.

I saw that on Shabbos one faces the self, unobstructed by weekday distractions which form a screen. I also began to see that the experience is more pleasurable for those who have achieved something of their potential during the previous week or during life in general; for those who have diffused their creative energy entirely into externalities and therefore depend on an artificial external world for the sensation of existence, facing themselves means facing emptiness; the experience is not pleasant and the weekend becomes an even more frenetic involvement in some or other form of escape.

This realm of transcendent existence is constructed by keeping the Shabbos laws; abstaining not from "work" as is usually understood, but from *melacha*, those thirty-nine categories of creative action by which the *mishkan* was built, and by kabbalistic inference since the *mishkan* is a microcosm of the universe, those actions with which Hashem created the world. On Shabbos, the day of intrinsic being, one abstains from that which defines the weekday, the process of creation, and enjoys the elevated state of completed creation, both of the world and of the self. This understanding and the experience itself answered a deep need in me at that time, the need for an opportunity to take stock regularly, to have a "time-out" from the whirl of medicine and everything else in order to keep in touch with myself, to maintain clarity and direction in the most aware way possible, and Shabbos, this amazing day of superconsciousness, was that opportunity.

---

mishkan: the Sanctuary   *Hashem:* lit. "the Name"; G-d

I fell in love with the atmosphere in that house, the relationships between parents and children and between the children themselves, the peace, the happiness. There was something living in that house besides the people, and it was palpable and almost visible. Once, much later, a child told me that she would see a big white bird that had flown all week flutter silently into her house on Shabbos evening and spread its wings over everything, and I knew exactly what she meant.

I began keeping Shabbos. My parents were always my inspiration, and their encouragement was of great importance to me. My mother arranged things so that I could observe it as I wished to, and my father and I began learning *chumash* together every Shabbos. Over a period of time the effect on us all was profound. I began learning gemara, keeping other *mitzvos*, and experienced a sense of direction. My sister, doing her own thinking and drawing her own conclusions about values in life, became observant and married a lawyer who had learned in Ohr Somayach.

One day soon after Yom Kippur my father called me. While running his busy specialist practice he had been reading about *Yiddishkeit* and finding time to attend *shiurim*, and he had something to tell me. "I imagined I received a letter from the bank," he said, "the bank of Heaven. It read: 'Dear Sir, As you are no doubt aware, at some future date we shall be obliged to close your books. We have been looking through your account of *mitzvos* and *aveiros*, and as you know, we are not permitted to disclose your balance; however, may we suggest that you consider making some new investments with us at this time.'

"So I've decided to start keeping Shabbos."

"JODE! VAL UIT!"

During my internship I began wearing a *kippa* and *tzitzis* to the surprise of my friends, most of whom had never thought the romance would ever get *that* serious. Some came with me and we

---

chumash: the Five Books of Moses   *gemara:* Talmud
mitzvos: commandments   *Yom Kippur:* Day of Atonement
aveiros: transgressions   *kippa:* skullcap, yarmulke
tzitzis: fringes hung on four-cornered garment

grew together, some rapidly decided that I was not as normal as they had previously thought. Most identified and even vaguely understood but had not had the personal experiences to motivate change in their own lives; some of them, when subsequently exposed to Torah and *Yiddishkeit*, became involved more rapidly than I had. I completed my internship and went to learn in the yeshiva of the Kollel community and it was during this phase that my wife and I (we were married at the start of my internship) became fully involved in the yeshiva community and I had my first taste of full-time learning, an experience I was to continue later in Jerusalem.

A few months later I was drafted for two years' compulsory service in the South African army as a medical officer and left home for a very unfriendly army barracks and basic training. The transition from yeshiva to the army was stark, to say the least; from being surrounded by people who were working on refining themselves and striving to become pure, dropped into the degradation of dirty jokes and filthy language which are staple army fare.

I had expected anti-semitism during the basic training and officer's course but observed an interesting phenomenon — the more openly observant a Jew was, the less likely was he to suffer abuse. Many times I heard "Jood" ("Jew" in Afrikaans) applied to a fellow recruit whom I hardly recognized as Jewish, but I was never the victim of so much as a comment, let alone curses, which represents remarkable *hashgacha pratis* in the context of an army training base. The image of a bearded, white-tassled Jew paradoxically generated respect whereas the ostensibly unidentifiable Jew was somehow identified for insults. Consistent with this principle, the only person I saw treated even more respectfully than myself was a *ba'al teshuva* colleague who was a *chassid*, never trimmed his beard, wore *peyos* and walked around the camp on Shabbos in his Shabbos suit and *kapata* (frock coat) scorning uniform, and was never reprimanded for this flagrant breach of military discipline. I think the sergeants and corporals in charge of our training were actually afraid to speak to him on Shabbos, although it is difficult to think of anything

---

hashgacha pratis: Divine providence at personal level   *peyos:* sidelocks

else that would have made those particular individuals afraid.

In fact, the entire period of my military service was an experience of direct *hashgacha* and an opportunity for growth in *emunah*. One Sunday during basic training the camp was assembled after "kerkparade'" (church parade) for a session known as "spiritual preparedness." The Afrikaans-speaking recruits were marched off to be addressed by one of their priests, and the Jews were ordered to go with the English speakers; since all of us spoke English the logic was that we should feel quite comfortable during the English-speaking priest's sermon. A priest with the rank of colonel began expounding his views of Scripture showing how everything held by his church was actually a direct and exact fulfillment of the Old Testament. Most of the arguments were transparent to even the least informed of us, although some were quite intriguing in their originality. Somehow however, we knew that he had to be openly refuted or we would all be sullied by what would be perceived as an acquiescence by our silence. Although I knew relatively little, I knew more than anyone else present and suddenly I felt all the Jewish eyes on me — when it came to an attack on Judaism from the outside, even the least observant was as committed as the rest, and if I had not spoken up, someone else would have. Fortunately, the "sermon" was easy to demolish.

In the ensuing silence I had visions of a court-martial or at least a permanent posting to the Okavango swamps, but the reaction was *min hashamayim* — the next Sunday morning, after the usual separation into groups, a new group was added: "Jode! Val uit!" ("Jews! Fall out!") We were sent off to the NCO's mess, located at the furthest possible point from both English *and* Afrikaans speakers, to see to our own "spiritual preparedness" however we saw fit, obviously beyond redemption! We organized a *shiur*, and once a week a Rosh Yeshiva would come out to the camp.

Some of the Jews in that group learned more in those *shiurim* than they had learned in their entire prior lifetimes. I was ordered by the camp commander to escort the Rabbi, and it was my joy,

---

hashgacha: Divine providence   *emunah:* faith
min hashamayim: from Heaven   *Rosh Yeshiva:* head of a yeshiva

apart from the *shiur* itself, to have to march alongside him through the camp — as his jet-black hat, long frock and silver mane of a beard swept by, heads would turn and silence fall until we were long past.

BATTLE ZONE

After being commissioned, I was posted to the South West African operational zone as a medical officer, and as the military transport dropped almost vertically out of the sky to avoid terrorist ground fire over Grootfontein, I was to begin a period of intense personal growth.

The trauma and death with which I had worked during my training had somehow never seemed personal, but here in South West everything seemed more serious. Firstly, there was a war going on. The day we arrived at operational headquarters, a friend of mine was killed. We had been classmates at medical school for six years; we received our postings together in the late afternoon of that first day in a command tent on the dusty outskirts of Grootfontein, and at the last moment, my orders were changed and I was sent to a different sector. We said goodbye and he boarded the flat-bed army truck with a group of doctors and other medical personnel and they moved out into the bush. Close to sunset they ran into a terrorist ambush. Most of the others on the truck were lying down, resting; he was sitting upright, looking out at the majesty of the African bush. He was hit in the chest and died before his friends could help him.

Secondly, I was no longer a junior working under the watchful eyes of experienced consultants — I was alone and responsible for my own patients for the first time.

I was given a medical ward in the large hospital at Katatura. This is the referral center for the whole territory and the patients in my ward represented the complicated and serious cases which could not be treated in the outlying areas, and included advanced cancers, brain abscesses and rare tropical conditions as well as the usual problems of tuberculosis and malnutrition-associated disease. More than once we found ourselves in the midst of a typhoid fever epidemic, and in fact the last experience I had there was connected with one of these: in my last week of duty we had two deaths from typhoid in the ward, and one night as I lay in bed, more exhausted than usual, I was surprised to feel something unusual in my abdomen — I palpated while inhaling and made the easy diagnosis — my spleen was grossly enlarged and I had typhoid. Reporting sick would have meant weeks in a military hospital instead of going home for Pesach, so I continued as normal for a few days until my leave fell due, suffering with my patients and learning invaluable lessons about how it feels to be a patient with a serious diagnosis.

A number of experiences changed me greatly during my six months at Katatura and deeply impressed upon me how the practice of medicine in difficult circumstances is translated into an effect on the *midos*, for better or for worse. One was the daily ward work; I would begin the morning ward round with the nurses and two interns who were my juniors and had even less practical experience than I had. Initially a feeling of panic would grip me as we moved from one seriously ill patient to the next — I held the final responsibility for each one; because of the military situation and uncertain future of South West there were no consultants in the wards and junior staff like myself had been put into the breach by the army. I had never treated a patient before except as an intern and had none of that confidence and practical intuition which come only with years of practice, and here I found myself treating some of medicine's most difficult problems.

I tried to make up for lack of knowledge by increased vigilance and effort, and I saw others respond to the situation in various ways. Two examples impressed themselves indelibly on my memory. On busy intake nights I was always faced with a personal dilemma; after working extremely long hours without a break and often without a meal, in the early hours of the morning I would search my conscience for a justification to get a few hours rest so that I could make responsible decisions the next day. If the patients were relatively stable I would leave their care in the hands of the interns,

---

Pesach: Passover   *midos:* character traits

who would have the following day off, with careful instructions, and go off for two or three hours' sleep — until something happened which changed my mind. One particularly busy night we had struggled to stabilize a young woman, who had respiratory problems, on oxygen. When she finally settled and began to recover I left her with the intern, leaving clear instructions for him to measure her arterial oxygen concentration hourly and to call me if anything changed. When I arrived for the post-intake round in the morning I found the intern comfortably asleep in bed and the patient in respiratory failure. He had simply not bothered to check on her at all and had no excuse to offer. She died under my hands on the way to the intensive care unit.

The other event was the arrival on the ward of a colleague of mine from Cape Town to assist me. His reaction was quite the opposite. His response to his own lack of knowledge and skill when faced with a difficult clinical situation when nothing more could be done was to stand at the bedside and simply watch the patient. He would remain there in a torment of frustration at the situation and our lack of ability to offer definitive help, and do nothing more than constantly monitor the vital signs and worry. He would continue thus until daylight, and more than once collapsed on the ward round. His stubborn refusal to delegate authority in order to rest for even a few minutes was a constant challenge to my solution of compromise, and I began to see more and more clearly how self-control and personality training are as essential to good medicine as the best technical skills.

I had noticed during my internship days that mistakes and poor judgment are more likely when doctors' personal *midos* like pride and anger get in their way than when more external factors such as work pressure and exhaustion are involved. My awakening to this was the experience of a close friend who had been assisting at a particularly difficult abdominal operation; the surgeon was struggling to expose the anatomy and had to stop frequently for the theater nurse to mop the sweat from his brow. The ever-present exhausted intern was holding a wound retractor, and when its position changed slightly, obscuring the surgeon's view, the surgeon lost his temper. Taking hold of the intern's hand he jerked the retractor in the abdominal wound with a stifled curse and prepared to continue, but froze instead. Everyone in the theater stared in horror at the patient's abdomen rapidly welling up with blood. The rest of the operation consisted of repairing a ruptured inferior vena cava while the anesthetist transfused unit after unit of standby blood. I had already been learning *mussar* and resolved to always keep calm under pressure, but it is not always easy, to say the least.

My own test came now. Apart from the ward work, it was the duty of every medical officer at Katatura to run the casualty department (or emergency room) once every few nights. There were sometimes thirty or forty patients waiting, mostly from the nearby township, a depressed socio-economic area, and I would arrive in a sweat of trepidation and rapidly scan the waiting line for cases which looked more serious. A casualty doctor's working rule is that those who are groaning or even screaming in pain are usually in less danger than the completely silent, and more than once I pulled in a semi-conscious, severely dehydrated baby for resuscitation ahead of those who were able to talk for themselves. Patients presented themselves through the night in a steady stream and I pitted my newly qualified and pitifully inexperienced skill against stabbings, fractures, acute abdomens and rapes; on a typical night I found myself inserting a drain into a stabbed chest in one room, managing a case of pulmonary edema in another, preparing at least one patient for emergency surgery at any given time, treating a puff-adder bite which was threatening to cause irreversible shock and fending off the inevitable drunks. I was much too busy to feel miserable and I was intoxicated with exhaustion and relief when dawn broke and I could drag myself upstairs to my quiet ward where the lung abscesses and leukemias seemed tame by comparison.

In the midst of all this very unspiritual chaos my wife arrived and transformed our small room into a home. Each week we hacked out a haven of Shabbos in that end-of-the-earth place, our candlelight spilled out into the South West African night, and we felt as if we were a microcosm of the *galus*, a small spark in the

---

mussar: Torah teaching on character development   *galus:* Diaspora

darkness of Africa. Late on Friday afternoons Jewish soldiers who were within reach would arrive to spend Shabbos with us, and as the unbelievable smell of baking *challos* wafted over us and the sun set over the hospital and the desert scrub beyond, the week seemed to melt into insignificance. We would talk *divrei Torah* and sing *zmiros* until late into the night, much to the surprise of our Afrikaans acquaintances who would look in and marvel at the scene of the glowing Shabbos table with fresh *challos*, candles and wine and our small band of happy Jews, singing as if this world had somehow become the next.

Two of our Shabbos guests ended up in yeshiva. One was a colleague of mine who had always been interested in *Yiddishkeit*; we began learning together on Shabbos and when his leave became due we suggested he visit our *kehilla* in Johannesburg on the way to his home in the Cape. We later heard that he had spent a Shabbos with the Rosh Yeshiva and subsequently returned to learn there. He and his family are still there; he learns half-day and works as an emergency room doctor to support his learning.

The other was an officer in an infantry unit who had the usual South African Jewish background and for whom the idea of learning in a yeshiva would have been unthinkable then. He had gone through infantry training and the subsequent officer's course in one of the toughest units in the army and was in charge of a section of a base near Windhoek. We could see the effect that the Shabbos experience had on him, but when he left the territory at the end of his service it was for a world trip before deciding what to do in life.

Some time later I received a card from Jerusalem:

"Am visiting Ohr Somayach Yeshiva. Have been here for two days, had a great time, am now leaving for Eilat with some friends and plan to go on to Europe."

Two months later a letter arrived. Postmark: Jerusalem.

"Well, I'm still at Ohr Somayach. It's been an amazing two months, which I'll never forget. I'm finally leaving for Eilat next week."

---

challos: Sabbath bread   *divrei Torah:* words of Torah
zmiros: Sabbath table songs   *kehilla:* community

One year later, in Johannesburg, I received another letter. It was also from Jerusalem, and it consisted of *divrei Torah*. When I arrived at Ohr Somayach he was still there, and we learned some Michtav Me-Eliyahu together before he left for his *chassuna* in the States, where he now learns.

After six months' duty in South West Africa I was posted close to home with the usual duties of a military doctor, and I had more time to learn. On completing my service I worked in general surgery for a few months until we were able to come to Jerusalem, where we arrived one year during Succos. At first I learned half-day in Ohr Somayach and later was able to learn full-time; and eventually joined the yeshiva's kollel, "Meshech Chochma Ohr Yehoshua."

ON THE DAF

Since I have become involved in learning, many people outside the yeshiva world ask me, "What exactly do you learn in yeshiva? What is gemara and why do you study it so intensively?" Really, you have to taste it to understand, but I explain what I can.

The Written Law (Chumash, the Five Books of Moses) contains the "what" of the *mitzvos;* it lays down all 613 *mitzvos,* and at a deeper level contains everything: Torah is conceived of as the "blueprint of the universe," this means that nothing can exist in the real world, either physically or conceptually, unless its source is in Torah. The Oral Law however, contains the "how" of the *mitzvos.* Knowing "what" a particular *mitzva* is would not be enough to enable one to implement it, there must be a practical manual which explains how to set about doing the *mitzvos,* and that manual of practical instruction is contained in the Oral Law. Rabbi Simcha Wasserman illustrates this by explaining that the elements of a nutritious meal are digestible only when cooked. The raw nutriments of the Written Law may be undigestible to us: the gemara represents the "cooking" of these elements by the intellect and produces an applicable result.

Michtav Me-Eliyahu: classic mussar work by Rabbi E. E. Dessler
chassuna: wedding   *Succos:* festival of Tabernacles   *daf:* page (of Talmud)

Talmud consists of Mishna and gemara. The Mishna, expressed in Hebrew, in its original form was given at Sinai, orally, at the same time as the Written Law. It contains every *halacha* of the Torah, although in an extremely compressed form — apart from what is explicit, much is woven into its structure, forming an organic entity of inexhaustible depth. The gemara, in Aramaic, is a logical analysis of the Mishna, bringing to the level of the explicit what is implicit in Mishna, and is therefore much longer — many pages of gemara may be required to express all that is contained in one Mishna. The effort to understand gemara is an effort to bring to light all that is contained in Mishna.

At different times in history oral Mishna and gemara were written down to avert the danger of their being altered by the action of time and the tortures of *galus*, but the form of their writing ensures that they remain oral — far from a cold listing of facts, they are recorded in a way which necessitates a transmission of understanding from *Rebbe* to *talmid*, an encoding of great beauty, paradoxically and perhaps impossible to explain to the uninitiated, a code which means that understanding of the meaning of the words is not enough — one can translate a *blatt gemara* accurately and not have any idea of what it means initially, and yet, when the light dawns and understanding comes, one finds that everything which is being conveyed is entirely in the words themselves, and the clearer the *sugya* becomes, the more one sees how it is locked into the words on the page in a riveted structure of sublime balance and poise.

Learning to discern this structure is the first stage; the beginner learns to track down the *shakla vetarya* or "give-and-take" which forms the backbone of the *sugya* and from which its depth of meaning will become apparent. This structure alone is of great beauty, often complex and yet often surprisingly simple — but a simplicity which reveals itself only after a honing of the tools of the intellect permits its clear delineation.

This is only the beginning, for one soon discovers that this clarity

---

rebbe: rabbi, teacher   *talmid:* student
blatt gemara: page of Talmud   *sugya:* conceptual unit within Talmud

is multidimensional — the great commentaries, say, of the Rishonim, often differ on its definition, and one suddenly sees that the same seemingly immutable structure, when viewed from another angle, looks entirely different and yet obeys all the rules of form and structure in its new shape as it did in its previous one. Often one must hold both (or more) in the mind's eye at once and when clarity in all the commentaries has been attained the experience is the intellectual equivalent of turning a multifaceted diamond in the light.

One may obtain the impression from this description that the processes involved are personal or arbitrary — actually they are tautly defined in the most exacting and disciplined way. The *sevaros* used leave nothing to vague assumption, all premises must be satisfied always and interweaving themes must all be consistent with each other as well as within themselves. Unlike the sequential logic of mathematics, the gemara often explores patently wrong avenues, sometimes to demonstrate their invalidity and always extracting truth in the process. The process of demolishing false arguments in order to establish the truth has been described as "uprooting mountains and grinding them together."

The system used to engage the gemara is one of *chavrusa;* two partners learn together in a lively exchange. The various possibilities inherent in the *sugya* often generate heated discussion, the *beis midrash* sounds like a battlefield in the "war of Torah," and often diametrically opposed views yield a synthesis of understanding which is impossible to achieve alone. One is often amazed after trying to decipher a gemara alone, how one is sparked off by a *chavrusa* and how between you the *sugya* comes alive and reveals its structure and its secrets.

Rav Wasserman once described a gemara *sugya* as a knot. It is a seemingly tangled piece of cord with apparently many loose ends, knotted into the smallest space possible; it can be disentangled only slowly, and when it has been completely freed, it shows itself to be simply one straight piece of string with only two ends.

Rishonim: Torah authorities of approx. 10th-15th centuries
sevaros: logical constructs   *chavrusa:* study partner

One can become enraptured with the clarifying of structure alone, but this is not all. The dissecting of the *sugya's* anatomy and micro-anatomy is done only in order to elucidate the deeper level, that of the underlying conceptual framework which is the physiology of the *sugya*, the understanding of how it works. The effort here is to trace the discussion to its common denominators, to find that unifying concept or theme which gives rise to the whole issue and explains its manifold structure. The effort demanded challenges the best minds and there is no limit to the depth which can be reached. It is breathtaking to have struggled for hours or days on a *sugya* until its elements and *sevaros* are etched on the mind and to have defined its structure and usually many unanswered questions, and then to hear a *shiur* from the Rosh Yeshiva and in a flash of clarity understand the connections and see down to the source.

Often the process is multistaged; basic understanding and difficulties, sudden insight which seems to explain everything, a minor question which suddenly becomes major when explored, nothing makes sense at all, more thought, new idea, deeper understanding and vastly new clarity and so on, and sometimes at the end of a long series of such efforts to crack open the shell of a *sugya*, one finds a word or two in a Rishon which takes in the whole road one has travelled. There is never a dull moment and only a full engagement of the intellect can yield success; one detail vaguely grasped and everything becomes vague. There is no way to describe the thrill of descending through the layers of a *sugya* to a level where one begins to understand what the Rishonim are saying and experiences the electricity holding everything together, the sparkle of each of the elements in the structure, their interdependence and range of consequences.

Beyond this lies the level of *chiddush* — the unique experience of becoming so identified with Torah that from the well of one's own being an original insight is drawn which sheds new light; the primordial inborn Torah in the essence of the self rising to consciousness.

---

chiddush: new thought

Understand also, that all this is not a process applied to irrelevant material — the stuff of which the *sugyos* consist is the very fabric of the world; the gemara deals with everything from personal duties to moral and ethical concepts, the nature and structure of the human psyche, interpersonal relationships, the metaphysical; in short, the universe. Depth in gemara is insight into the universe. Elucidating the multidimensional structure of gemara *sugyos* is a training to see reality in its different cross-sections. Gemara requires a fine sensitivity, reality is subtle. A journey through a *masechta* is an ocean voyage, one visits exotic islands, meets beautiful and fearsome creatures — often oneself (as the case may be!) and experiences discovery on every page; as Rabbi Nota Schiller puts it in his *shiurim* on *Torah shebe'al peh* "floating on the *daf*" through the ages of Jewish history and this world, and sometimes even peeping into the next.

Actually, there is much more than this rhapsody of form and content. The letters which comprise the root of the word "Mishna" (משנה) also spell "*neshama*," the soul, "*shmoneh*" the number eight, and "*shemen*," oil. The intrinsic connection between these ideas is that they all have to do with the meeting of the material with the spiritual. Eight is the number which denotes transcendence beyond the physical (seven forms the basis of the physical world — seven days in the physical creation, seven colors in the spectrum, seven different notes in the musical scale), and oil is that which the wick draws in order to give a flame (*ner Hashem nishmas adam* — "A candle of Hashem is the soul of man"; the candle is a symbol of the human — the wick represents the body and the flickering flame the *neshama*, the oil forms their interface). All of this is rooted in the word "Mishna" because Mishna represents the point of contact between Hashem and the expression of His Oral Law in the world; the primal condensation of the Oral Law from its Divine dimension of origin at the giving of the Torah was into the form of the Mishna; the gemara represents a further bringing down into a more concrete and tangible form. This means that the endeavor of learning gemara, which is to understand the Mishna as a seminal root, is in fact

---

masechta: tractate of Talmud   *Torah shebe'al peh:* the Oral Law   *neshama:* soul

a reaching up to the highest level of reality, an involvement with the most rarefied and potent expression of Hashem's will in the Oral Law, the *neshama* of *Torah shebe'al peh*.

This also opens a chink of understanding into an amazing gemara: Rebbe (Rabbi Yehuda HaNasi), who compiled the Mishna in its present form, commanded that after his death a bed should be made, a candle lit, and the table laid in his house on *erev Shabbos* and later, after leaving this world, he would come back in human form, body and soul together, on *erev Shabbos*. He would go home and make *kiddush*, and was clearly visible to human eyes. Apart from the more obvious questions, why Rebbe and no-one else? And why specifically on *erev Shabbos?* Because Rebbe, more than any other mortal, *was* Mishna; and just as Mishna reflects the force of connection between body and soul of the *Torah shebe'al peh*, Rebbe was himself part of this force. Therefore putting together body and soul, even after leaving the usual realm of their unity, was of his essence. And on *erev Shabbos*, because that is the very same concept in the dimension of time; *bein hashmashos*, twilight of *erev Shabbos* when the week becomes the Shabbos, is the interface between the physical organism of the week and its soul, that wisp of *olam haba* which is the Shabbos.

✻ ✻ ✻

Gemara comprises two sections — *halacha* and *aggada*. *Halacha* deals with the application of *mitzvos*, the legal in its broadest sense. *Aggada* includes all the rest — deep discussions of the roots of existence, the mystical — and it requires additional tools in order to be understood. Rabbi Wasserman's advice to the broken-hearted student who cannot fathom a particular piece of *aggada* is to leave it, learn gemara for a few more years and then to try again. That *aggada* is like the fine machinery of a delicate watch, and the student has only plumber's tools at his disposal. With plumber's tools he will smash it, and the only way of refining the coarse tools of the mind is to learn more Torah. In Rav Wasserman's words, "Gemara is a brain-grinding tool." Later, when the tools have become

---

erev Shabbos: day before the Sabbath   *Kiddush:* Sabbath sanctification over wine
bein hashmashos: twilight   *olam haba:* the world to come

sufficiently refined, he will be able to take that *aggada* apart and reconstruct it without damage. This is one reason why the wisdom of Kabbala is couched in secrets. Its correct understanding is possible only by a powerful-enough mind; an improperly prepared recipient may be irreparably damaged, and so it is clothed in many covers. Correctly guided, one can learn worlds from the very coverings themselves, and this suffices while the vessel is being prepared for deeper content.

The grapple with gemara is difficult at every level of expertise. It is exhausting even physically. During my first months in yeshiva I would come home daily more deeply exhausted than I had been as an intern, if that is possible to imagine. The preparation of a university degree is almost irrelevant, the intellectual level demanded in yeshiva learning makes university study pale into insignificance and this is the experience of university graduates who come to yeshiva from technical and theoretical faculties alike, medicine and engineering, or philosophy — none seems able to prepare the critical intellectual abilities required adequately. I recall my first day in yeshiva clearly — I was a little offended at being assigned an eighteen year-old *chavrusa;* after all, I thought, I was a man of the world, university graduate, had studied medicine as well as literature, and similar inflated thoughts, and here was a high school graduate to match wits with me. At any rate, I could not keep up with him. Not at all. In fact I felt like giving up — was I so stupid? His mind was so extended by his years of gemara training while I was being fooled by the illusion that at university I was learning to think, that there was no comparison between us. The whole of the first week was a painful experience — every question I asked he either answered immediately or patiently showed me how a little thought would reveal it not to be a question at all. I discovered that he and his contemporaries learned gemara most of the day at high school and achieved distinctions in the secular matriculation examinations although they devoted a short session only at the end of the day to secular studies — in other words, if one develops the young mind correctly, the syllabus of a secular high school is laughable in terms of difficulty and can be easily mastered in a minimum of time. I consoled myself later by recalling that he went on to become one of the best in the Ponovezh Yeshiva, but it did not prevent a rude awakening then. What a tragedy that secular education deprives its children of the opportunity to develop even a fraction of their true greatness.

Many times since then I have sat opposite a *chavrusa* who is new to yeshiva. He has heard of the challenge of gemara, and he is thinking how his doctorate in philosophy from Stanford will wipe out my irrelevant medical degree and presumably my inconsequential years poring over these old pages too. We begin learning, and as I patiently repeat the explanation of the *sugya* and watch his ego shrink, I remember how it feels.

Parents in the non-Torah world, however, have quite the opposite impression. They feel that their *ba'al teshuva* children in yeshiva are performing some limited esoteric exercise and forever missing the opportunity to become intellectual giants at university. A distressed mother asked a certain Rosh Yeshiva what she could do about her brilliant son who had chosen to stifle his intellect in a yeshiva and received the quiet reply: "Let him try yeshiva. If he drops out, he can become a nuclear physicist."

Children in Torah education are not only stimulated intellectually, however. On the contrary, the emphasis is on growing up to be a "*mensch*" in every sense. A teacher who became a *ba'alas teshuva* once told me how amazed she was when she began teaching the youngest class at the yeshiva school in Johannesburg. On the wall alongside the merit star charts for good spelling and arithmetic were similar charts for good *midos* — kindness to others, for example sharing lunch with a child who had none, and other measures of character development. And why not? If a child's progress is monitored in spelling and arithmetic but not in character building, he gets the idea that only the former are important. Hence a Torah education includes education for life in general, for friendships, for marriage, in short, for everything, because Torah *is* everything. Secular education gives instruction in language, mathematics,

mensch: lit. "person"; decent human being

computers and many other technical areas but leaves the young person to grope for himself when it comes to the really important subject of preparation for life as a "*mensch.*"

As in all endeavors, one measures one's development against models who have accomplished, and it is here that one sees the results of Torah learning. Contact with *gedolei* Torah dispels any doubt about the quality of the finished product and provides an ideal of breathtaking grandeur. Firstly, intellectually. A visit to a *gadol* for advice or help with a personal problem is illuminating. I had the experience of arriving to discuss a difficult problem with a certain Rosh Yeshiva, and while I was formulating my introduction, he kindly took over, stated my problem briefly and exactly, and then gave the solution; and subsequently I have become used to it. The clarity of insight, sharpness in defining the issues and chopping out irrelevancies, and intuition at fitting the solution to the individual are familiar to young people in the yeshiva world.

One of the most impressive aspects is that of memory. I had heard of people knowing *shas* (the whole Talmud — many tractates in many volumes) and commentaries by heart but never really believed it until I saw it, again and again. One young Rav who is a *posek* in Jerusalem occasionally asks me what I am learning, and whatever I answer — and I answer only by quoting the *masechta* and page number — he tells me what is of particular importance on that page and which commentaries to see.

Some time ago a well-known Rosh Yeshiva visited our kollel, and asked the Rosh Kollel where we had begun learning that *zman*. The Rosh Kollel quoted the page number only and the Rosh Yeshiva immediately fired through the gemara by heart from that page to the end of the *perek*, eight *blatt*, at high speed, simultaneously mentioning outstanding features of the Rashi and Tosefos.

What is even more amazing, though, is to hear these men talk of *their* Roshei Yeshiva of the previous generation in terms that make it clear that their own abilities are minor in comparison with

---

gadol, gedolei Torah: man or men great in Torah   *Rav:* rabbi
posek: halachic authority   *zman:* semester   *perek:* chapter
Rashi: famous 11th century Torah commentator
Tosefos: later medieval commentaries

the power of learning that existed only one generation ago. Rabbi Yisroel Salanter, the founder of the modern *mussar* movement, was once scheduled to give a *shiur klali* in the yeshiva. On his way to the podium, he noticed that the list of references for the *shiur* posted on the *beis midrash* wall had been changed to a haphazard set of references by an element which intended to show failings in his policy of introducing the study of *mussar* — his *shiur* would be on a topic completely irrelevant to the references which the misled students had researched. He paused briefly in front of the sabotaged list (which typically refers to sources all over the gemara, the commentaries through the ages, and the major halachic works), proceeded to the podium and gave a *shiur* on *those* references! And the brief pause was not to recall the sources but rather to weigh the question of whether giving such a *shiur* would be too prideful or not, before deciding that it had to be done.

But memory is only a tool, and more exciting is to glimpse the depth of the Torah mind. A great man whose *shiurim* I have been privileged to attend would give a private *shiur* on *motza'ei Shabbos* to five or six *avreichim*. There was no set topic, and he would ask what everyone wanted to hear. Each *talmid* would state a topic, which generally ranged from the weekly *sedra* to a request for an explanation of the mystical concept of the *succah shel livyasan*, all completely diverse and disparate topics. He would think for a moment and then give a *shiur* on *one single theme* which was the *essence* of all the topics requested. On one occasion he explained that this was possible because all of Torah is one unity; each of its 613 aspects contains all the 612 others within itself, which means that lack of understanding of even one detail means a lack of proper understanding of everything because any other aspect will be lacking that of its facets which is this one distant detail; and conversely, a deep enough understanding of Torah yields a knowledge of the points of contact between any of its parts.

But more important even than this is the development of the personality, the human being as a whole, the "*mensch*," which one

---

shiur klali: comprehensive lecture   *motza'ei Shabbos:* Saturday night
avreichim: kollel students   *sedra:* Torah portion
succah shel livyasan: succah made of the skin of leviathan

sees in people who learn Torah. One sees the face change; a face full of ta'avah enters the yeshiva, it shows unmistakably, and it changes and radiates as its owner absorbs the purity of Torah. Once again, the greats show the way — the great men of Torah time and again, through their learning of Torah and *mussar* and their concentration on character building and self-control, provide examples of superhuman achievement.

Rabbi Moshe Feinstein was being escorted in New York on a particular occasion, when after being helped into the car, he asked the driver not to proceed. After a long pause, when the person who had helped him was no longer in sight, Rav Feinstein opened the car door and removed his hand which had been caught by the door and the fingers smashed. The amazed driver asked, "Rebbe, why didn't you scream?" He had not uttered a sound. Rav Feinstein replied: "I did not want to embarrass the person who closed the door on my hand."

And this humility is at the center of the Torah personality. When my Rosh Yeshiva rose to speak at my *chassuna* the spontaneous comment of one of the guests was "He seems to borrow the space he walks in." And it is not a veneer, it is the core: the Brisker Rov once explained why the Chofetz Chaim, the greatest Torah sage of the last generation, was known in his own lifetime as a *tzaddik* but not, relatively speaking, as a sage: because he *davened* that his Torah-knowledge should not be apparent. So why did he not *daven* that he should remain hidden as a *tzaddik* too? Said the Brisker Rov: "The Chofetz Chaim never requested that he remain hidden as a *tzaddik, because he did not know that he WAS one!*"

Someone who learns Torah *li'shma,* for its own sake with no vested interest, is *zoche lidvarim harbei* — merits to be granted the knowledge of "many things." Apart from intellect and character, a deep study of Torah yields knowledge about that replica of Torah which is the Universe. What kinds of knowledge? I shall record just one example, from the medical field, although I have personally experienced the amazing on a number of occasions while working

---

ta'avah: lit. "desire"; involvement in the physical
Chofetz Chaim: Rabbi Yisroel Meir Hacohen Kagan of Radin
tzaddik: righteous individual   daven: pray

medically in contact with *gedolei* Torah.

The great Chazon Ish was famed for a knowledge of medical matters, although he had no formal medical training. In one well-known case, a mother took her son to the Chazon Ish because he had been diagnosed as having a lethal brain tumor. It had been decided to operate, although the attempt was desperate since safe access to the tumor seemed almost impossible. The Chazon Ish gave the boy a *bracha*, told the mother that all would be well, and gave her a diagram which he had drawn for the neurosurgeon concerned. The diagram indicated a surgical approach to the tumor and technique of operation. Now most doctors do not like being told what to do, especially surgeons, and especially by Rabbis, but the mother did as she was told and presented the diagram. The neurosurgeon looked at it and immediately admitted that it represented the only possibility of successful surgery. The tumor was removed and the boy recovered. The surgeon subsequently made the following comment to a friend of one of my teachers: "That the Chazon Ish knows more Torah than I do, I understand. *But how does he know more neurosurgery?*"

Chazon Ish: Rabbi Avraham Yeshaia Karelitz, of Lithuania and later Bnei Brak
bracha: blessing

On Eagles' Wings

Israelis are different. Their more labile Mediterranean temperament makes their responses more radical and those who experiment with Eastern and other cults generally do so more intensively than their Anglo-Saxon counterparts. Likewise, their *teshuva* is different — often much more rapid and involving individuals one would less likely predict as candidates for *teshuva*. Over the past couple of years Israeli society has been deeply affected by the *"chozer beteshuva"* movement and amazed articles dot the secular press documenting the movement of top Israeli intellectuals, entertainers and others into the yeshiva world. Whereas an American may take weeks, or a South African months, to consider changing his lifestyle, an Israeli is likely to change overnight and become immediately more radically opposed to his previous frame of reference, often vehemently so.

My friend Allon was a pilot in one of the Israeli Air Force's crack squadrons. After five years as a combat pilot, flying the beefed-up Israeli version of the U.S.-made Skyhawk (11,500 pounds thrust; standard is 9,500 pounds) he began to wonder about spirituality. In Israel until recently this was unusual — Air Force pilots occupy perhaps the most admired position in society and are universally respected as the pinnacle of the military pyramid. Their training is the toughest and only the very best make the grade; and of those

teshuva: rediscovery of Torah Judaism
chozer beteshuva: current Israeli usage for *ba'al teshuva*

who finally earn their wings, only the best of these become interceptor and fighter pilots, and theoretically at least, the young man in his early twenties who earns his seat in a Phantom or Skyhawk has everything — rank, glory and the unlimited admiration of girls.

After riding this wavecrest for five years, the sensitive side of Allon's nature began to awaken. During his training he had had little time to think — beginning military service as a teenager, the route to the top had been a hard grind of physical and emotional exertion. Even during the most dangerous part of the flying training, aerial combat or dogfight practice which in modern supersonic fighters is a razor's-edge exercise of reflexes, he had been concentrating purely on how well he could do the job; and the only philosophical moment he had experienced was a split-second during the Litani campaign over Lebanon when a ground-to-air missile streaked across his cockpit windshield, inches in front of his nose. He told me that he had reacted with surprise: "They're trying to kill me!" he had muttered, almost as if he had not known it before; but apart from that he had been too busy.

He attended a *shiur*, had more questions, sought out a religious friend who steered him to a Rabbi for answers, attended a few more *shiurim*, and decided that his life was empty. He took six months' leave from the Air Force in order to learn in Ohr Somayach and at the end of this period decided to sign out for a longer leave. Apart from his friends in yeshiva, no-one quite believed it — who gives up that most sought-after position for some old books? But he was one of the first in a steady stream of military personnel who have come to Torah. He subsequently married a girl who had been with him in the Air Force as an air traffic controller and who had also become Torah observant.

When Allon took leave from the Air Force he was required to present himself for an interview with his commanding officer, the head of his air base with the rank of major-general.

The general came right to the point.

"What's this business about taking leave to learn? You're one

---

shiur(im): lecture(s)

of our best pilots; we've already taught you everything you need to know — what else is there to learn?"

No-one becomes an Air Force general by beating about the bush.

"You're wrong," Allon answered. "I've discovered that to ensure the survival of my people I need to know more than how to fly a Skyhawk."

Israeli *chutzpah.*

Allon told me some time later that in that phase of his development, shortly after choosing Torah, he could not believe that anyone else had not. His singleminded Israeli nature asserted itself as an extreme egocentricity — "This way of life is obviously correct, so why doesn't this general and everyone else see it?"

The general showed no emotion, but later confided to Allon's former squadron-leader that Allon's reply had been a blow below the belt. Incidentally, that squadron-leader soon afterwards also came to yeshiva.

As Allon was about to leave the room, and the air base, the general asked him a final question:

"Didn't you get anything from your experience here? After all, we brought you up — made you a pilot; surely you benefited in some way?"

"Yes," said Allon slowly, his blue eyes deepening in thought. "I did, I gained more than the privilege of fighting to defend Jews. If I would have been a paratrooper, running over rough ground, eating sand all the time, I might have looked up at the Skyhawks and thought: maybe a paratrooper needs *teshuva*, his life is hard, but those boys in the jets have everything, they certainly don't need *teshuva.* Or if I were a tank commander, sweating away in a clanking metal cabin, I might have thought the same: the pilots streaking overhead in the Phantoms have reached the ultimate — they surely don't need *teshuva.*

"But now that I've flown those jets I *know* that's not fulfillment. So you've helped me a lot."

Israelis are different.

---

chutzpah: cheek

Fundamentals and Parables

FOUNDATION

Andy is very serious. He had put aside all the big existential questions in order to study a profession, and now as a qualified accountant, he had left Johannesburg for Jerusalem to find out. As we sat down in the *beis midrash* during the *"chavrusa"* program, in which a beginner is paired with a more experienced partner, he pulled out a list of questions — he would write down his questions and often the answers too, and file them. Being Jewish, he had decided to start with Judaism, but planned to subsequently investigate as many religions and spiritual systems as possible and then draw up a balance sheet. He was serious about it and fully intended to commit himself to the winning option.

So I was Defender of the Faith.

He began his list: "Is there an Absolute? How do we know? Why can't we perceive it directly? How can a universe which is limited to the physical dimensions be evidence of a non-physical reality? If there is something out there, how do we know that the Jewish version of the truth is the correct one? Why should it obligate me?" There were a lot more questions as well. I said, "Well, I'm not sure we can discuss them all this evening, but let's make a start." He looked a little disappointed at the thought that enlightenment might

beis midrash: study hall   *chavrusa:* study partner

take longer than a company audit, but leaned forward with a frown of concentration.

We had met and spoken before, and I knew his position on most of these issues; only later I discovered his deep conviction that there is more to life than meets the eye, and that he had predicated much of his personal morality on this belief, but at that time, perhaps for the sake of testing the matter thoroughly, he articulated an uncommitted stance.

It was that of many young people and in fact forms the broad basis of the current agnostic or atheistic ambience in the West: since there seems to be no immediate evidence for anything beyond the finite, there probably is none; a corollary of this is that there is no ultimate meaning. Human beings are evolved forms of "lower" beings, our higher emotions and even intimations of a "Beyond" are only evolutionary survival devices or even non-functional anomalies of a random process.

The concept of a soul, however, is uncomfortable because it necessarily implies transcendence and suggests immortality, both of which challenge the finite view of the universe. The idea of a soul-body dichotomy is therefore rejected and whatever the soul is conceived to be, if it is admitted to exist at all, is usually expressed as being part of and indivisible from the physical body. This is another way of saying that a human being is no more than a finite physical entity, yet without totally denying him some higher capacity, namely, that area of the being which hopes, loves, desires to achieve, thinks abstractly and so on. There is thus an unavoidable acknowledgment of a "higher" functioning and of the paradoxical fact that we take our emotions seriously although we "know" that they are no more than electro-chemical brain activity which is supposedly purely the result of evolutionary chance. We "resolve" the paradox by asserting that these emotions and similarly the abstract concepts of truth, justice, beauty, honor and so on are meaningful despite the fact that they have no absolute dimension because we give them meaning. In fact, the only meaning in life is that with which we invest it; we create meaning.

We are bound by a pragmatic morality which is basically

expressed as: Do whatever you want as long as you do not limit anyone else's similar freedom; where possible, maximize freedom. In practice this means that one has strong rights, namely, to maximize freedom, but minimal obligations, namely, to desist from harming others; and even this simple obligation, since there is no absolute right and wrong, is only a necessary condition for reciprocity — it must be observed by the individual so that his freedom from harm by others is ensured. This focus on rights is a focus on the individual — my rights are due to *me* (whereas obligations turn the focus from the individual outwards), therefore the whole structure is based on the centrality of the self and hedonism is virtually its definition. There is no ultimate accountability and no eternal continuity; since this short life is all there is, the hedonism becomes all the more urgent.

I suggested that this garbled mess of a non-paradigm which is today's impoverished fare would reveal its crude falsehood when its elements are teased apart and analyzed. It is not held by young people because they have derived it intellectually; no-one sat down and thought it out — only an intellectual insect would present such a bundle of inconsistencies as a unified system; rather it is the passive result of vested interests and non-thought. The vested interests (alias the *yetzer hara*) are not intellectually demanding, they are easily satisfied by any framework which allows the individual to feed his desires and be the focus of his own universe. Rigorous logic is not mandatory.

Even for those who are not completely numbed by the environmental and media bombardment of one-dimensional inanity and do require an intellectually honest examination of the world, the battle to live differently is formidable. Often, mature appraisals of the falsehood of the whole structure remain in the realm of the intellect — the *yetzer hara* is expert at uncoupling insight and action, and even honest intellectuals (as opposed to those who are defeated at a prior stage of the battle and succumb to rationalizing their self-centeredness) often do not live according to their own analyses. Paradoxically, this does not always generate a sense of failure, on

---

yetzer hara: negative inclination

the contrary, there is a satisfaction in the intellectual sphere, and the elementary principle of consistency of thought and deed is overlooked.

* * *

Over the weeks we began to dismantle and reconstruct these issues from first principles. The first question was: Is there an Absolute or not? In other words, does Hashem exist? And how does one approach this issue? Now there are only three possible answers: Yes, No, or Maybe. The unadulterated egocentricity required to answer a confident "No" precludes further discussion — such a person's only claim against the existence of a transcendent reality is that it is (apparently) unprovable, but of course this does not amount to proof that it does *not* exist; his position is equally unprovable, and yet despite this he regards it as definite, therefore there is nothing more to say. One can only deal with logic. One who believes he can be certain about this option is either a fool or willfully evil, and both of these categories exclude themselves from any claim on our time. Also, beyond the smugness here, there is an intellectual problem involved if one claims to believe in the non-existence of any higher reality, since there can be no meaning if there is no absolute. "Meaning" is a term the definition of which is inseparable from a concept of transcendence; "meaning" is an abstract, which is to say that it is *beyond* the physical dimensions; therefore if there were only the immediate physical world with no dimension transcending it, it would by definition be meaningless. The idea that one can "create" meaning is a contradiction in terms; all this delusion amounts to is imagining a higher dimension, but the finite can of course never create the infinite, any "values" held by adherents of this position are no more than projections of the self and any moralizing beyond the barest utilitarianism is ridiculous. An existence in such a conceptual ethos is purely animal and it would be far more honest to admit it.

Part of this syndrome of fabricating realities is the often-heard response to religion: "If you believe, then it's true for you." Translated into practical terms this means that since I choose

Hashem: lit. "the Name"; G-d

not to believe, I negate the objective reality — it does not exist; but you, since you choose to believe, create that same reality which I have just destroyed. Of course this really means that there is no objective fact at all. Such idiocy is carried further — since you believe, you are obligated by the imperatives of the Divine, and you reap their reward and suffer punishment for their transgression, but since I want no part of these obligations and neither the reward nor the punishment, I am exempt! such is the non-intelligence of a culture steeped in unreality.

* * *

The honest and logical answer for a beginner is: "Maybe! I do not know!" and this was Andy's initial response. This needs careful thought. It means that there may be Hashem, G-d, the Absolute. How should one relate to this possibility? There are two possible attitudes:

(1) Since it is possible that Hashem exists, I choose to relate as if He does, and to live my life accordingly;

(2) Although it is possible, I choose to deny this possibility in practical terms; to live as if there is no ultimate accountability and no life after this.

What are the consequences, in this world and the putative next, of each of these two responses? Consider them in turn. Each has two possible outcomes, namely, either one turns out to be right, or wrong. Now what are the consequences of being right or wrong in either case? The theoretical possibility of being wrong in (1) or right in (2), that is that there might turn out to be no existence transcending this and therefore no life after this one, leaves one with a comparison of religious and non-religious lifestyles considered in this world only, which an experiential approach may clarify — living in the secular world and then in a Torah home and community answers this question for most who try it *even disregarding* the issue of a world to come.

But the big stakes lie elsewhere: in being right in (1) or wrong in (2), that is, right or wrong in the eventuality that there *does* turn out to be an Absolute! There can be no greater imaginable chasm — if one has chosen (1) and turns out to be right about it there is no greater success. The reward is eternity, a payoff beyond description or imagination. And if one says: so much for the next world, but what about the lifestyle required in this one which is a necessary part of the deal? It should be simple to see that even if this path involved difficulty and limitation in this world, even the greatest imaginable unpleasantness for an entire lifetime, it would be worthwhile since a lifetime is insignificant compared to the eternity that follows. Actually however, as already noted, a Torah lifestyle yields boundless benefit in this world too, as the *ba'alei teshuva*, those who have tried both options, testify.

However, if one has chosen (2) and turns out to be wrong about it the consequences are unspeakable. There can be no greater suffering, no greater loss; the loss of intrinsic eternal existence. The agony of this mistake is too chilling to grasp fully, but any faint awareness of its enormity is a beginning of insight into the concept of *gehinnom*.

Now there is an unknowable split of the probabilities, and the stakes are infinitely high — *can you afford to gamble?* It takes no great intellect to see that since the possibility of a Divine undeniably exists and one stands to gain or lose literally everything, one would be rash indeed to live a life which completely denies the maybe-yes option. And to *partly* accept in an attempt to cover one's bets may not be good enough — there is obviously only one way to relate to an Absolute: on *its* terms, not yours.

There are far nobler motivations for studying Torah, but this "doubt hypothesis" should be more than enough to motivate even the least aspiring.

Yet so many people ignore this cosmically important option and bet wildly in the greatest gamble that there is. To suggest that we relate seriously to hard visible facts only and not to possibilities is inadequate; the universal human response to the possibility of some immediate danger is extreme caution — if a room is thought to *possibly* contain a dangerously poisonous snake, for example, one enters, if at all, only with elaborate precautions and great trepidation;

---

ba'alei teshuva: those engaged in rediscovering Torah Judaism
gehinnom: dimension of retribution in the hereafter

in fact, the normal imagination *magnifies* the possibility of danger until it approaches certainty. And if the room were thought to contain some unknown, unspecified danger, the horror increases. Yet the ultimate danger, the greatest Unknown, is blithely ignored! The *yetzer hara* is a great persuader.

FAITH

But Andy wanted to know if there is a more positive, a more fundamental approach. Can the question concerning the existence of the Absolute ever be answered with the third option, a definite Yes? And if it could, would people not find themselves forced to live accordingly? We discussed a classic formulation of this question concerning *emunah:* How can *emunah* ever be meaningful — the existence of Hashem is either definitely knowable, or it is not. If it is ultimately knowable with a definite unequivocal clarity, then *emunah* does not exist — one does not have to believe in that which one knows; faith necessarily implies absence of certainty. On the other hand, if Hashem's existence is not knowable objectively, then *emunah* is foolish and purely arbitrary — one might choose to believe in anything, and it would make no more sense to believe in any particular purported reality than in any other; in fact it could be argued that the less likely the existence of the object of one's *emunah*, the greater the act of faith would be since it would receive less support from the rational intellect. At any rate, faith would be no more than an arbitrarily focused emotion. So what is the Jewish concept of *emunah?*

Andy chewed on this question for a long time and expressed the feeling that his entire relationship with Torah rested on a meaningful answer. I told him what Rabbi Simcha Wasserman had said on this subject and his face lit up with joy.

The Torah approach to this question is that firstly, the existence of Hashem is knowable. In fact the goal of development in Torah is to come to this knowledge rationally, and ultimately, experientially, and Torah learning is therefore a training in ruthless

---

emunah: faith

objectivity. Of course this is quite the opposite of the popular concept that "religion" requires a "leap of faith" to accept tenets which are never provable. Now we have two avenues of access to the knowledge of Hashem's existence. Firstly and more importantly, we met Him. Our Fathers stood at Sinai and experienced a Revelation which left no doubt — the potency and clarity of that Revelation were indescribably great, and it must be studied deeply in order to achieve even the beginning of an understanding of the magnitude of what happened. Among other important factors to consider is the fact that all the Jews alive at that time experienced the Revelation, whereas in all prior and subsequent history no revelation of the Absolute has so much as been purported to have been experienced by more than one individual alone. This means that even the outright liars (and *someone* must be lying since the fundamentals of the world's religions are by their own accounts mutually exclusive) never felt able to claim corroboration of a "revelation" by *even one* witness, while the Jews have handed down an undiluted tradition detailing a simultaneous and identical Revelation by everyone present, millions of people in number. Apart from the fact that all subsequent "prophets" of all religions have unreservedly accepted this original Revelation and its documentation, the Torah, while mutually excluding each other's additions to it, it was fundamentally different from anything mankind has ever experienced, either before or after. There is much more to be said here and these observations represent only the barest beginnings of some of the points discussed in the sources.

But what about us personally, Andy wanted to know, today's generation, far distant from Sinai? This experience is only hearsay for us; therefore the veracity and accuracy of its transmission to us become critically important. Once again, there are many factors to study. Firstly, the timespan. One tends to imagine the chain of transmission from Sinai stretching back into the vague past over innumerable generations. But a transmission over some 3,200 years requires only 80 generation or transmission periods of 40 years each ($80 \times 40 = 3,200$) — this means that heuristically speaking one can consider approximately 80 phases in which children or grandchildren received direct personal accounts of the tradition from their parents or grandparents, a number much smaller than usually appreciated. Also, there is unequivocal evidence that the transmission has been identical in all places and at all times, nothing like a mutable and ever-changing folk tradition — Torah scrolls of all communities in the world and excavated from all periods of history are identical.

And the transmission has not only been perfect, it has been potent. So seminal and incendiary was the original Revelation-experience that it ignited Jewish blood in a fire which has sparked off each generation until very recently to the degree that the overwhelming majority of Jews everywhere were prepared to give their lives en masse rather than even pretend to accept any alternative. Communities of people burned to death in their *shuls* rather than countenance the simple expedient of kissing a crucifix and going home; this level of commitment, in a people who are by their nature critically questioning, original, and proverbially unlikely to accept anyone else's opinion without an argument, and moreover who love life passionately by nature and by Torah-training, reflects the heat of a unique tradition searing through history and unparalleled by anything.

Also, one has to study each link in this chain of transmission, the people in each of the 80-odd "generations" who were its guardians. We know who they were; we know their greatness by historical account and we have their original works; we can pinpoint the handing over of the Torah-tradition from one almost superhuman luminary to the next, a multi-threaded wick through time which can be microscopically examined. This is no vague tale with its origins in the mists of time, it is a concrete, crystallized letter-by-letter whole, corroborated many times over at any point in its path, transmitted by people of a quality and dependability which are beyond description; we can and constantly do scrutinize the record and find it complete. (An appreciation of the greatness of the Torah-masters of each generation requires an understanding of the principle of *yeridas hadoros,* the relative descent of each era

---

shuls: synagogues

of generations in Jewish history in terms of spiritual greatness, which means that we are no more than the "sole of the foot" relative to the stature of earlier generations and from which we can begin to infer their level in order to grasp the personal greatness and integrity of these links in the Torah chain.)

To fully grasp the meaning of this transmission one must also consider the possibility of its having been forged. Assume for a moment that no historic gathering at Sinai occurred and that no Revelation ever took place. This would mean that the Torah-account of these events is a fabrication. At what point in history was this fabrication conceived and foisted on the Jewish people? Which generation of Jews unanimously took it upon themselves to convey a lie to their children with no trace of dissent? As pointed out already, two Jews seldom share one opinion on anything, and here we are suggesting that *all* Jews decided to perpetrate and perpetuate an enormous lie and yet we have no trace of even one admission that the whole thing was false. The unavoidable conclusion, no matter how uncomfortable for the sceptic, is that *if it were not true it would be impossible to fabricate and propagate.* Amazingly, it is easier to accept a Revelation of the Divine in terms of probability analysis than it is to postulate the peculiar sociological phenomenon of its having been fabricated and falsely transmitted by the whole Jewish nation with absolute conviction.

✳ ✳ ✳

So we are in possession of a documentation of the personal accounts of millions of witnesses who met Hashem in the most direct and immediate way possible, of surprisingly definable reliability. There is, however, a second way of coming to know of Hashem's existence — by considering the Universe.

Coming to understand the inevitability of a non-physical source for the finite is a science and is delineated in Torah classics which deal specifically with this issue. This was the method used by Avraham Avinu — working without a revelation he developed an understanding of the existence of the transcendent from deep and acute insight into the physical universe. This method is still valid

---

Avraham Avinu: our forefather Abraham

and necessary (but may be dangerous — the mind of Avraham Avinu was a tool of unsurpassed accuracy and reliability, but our intellects, easily warped by our lower selves and contaminated by an environment of unbridled insensitivity to these matters, may not be powerful enough).

However, there is an important caveat in this line of thinking: all methods of intellectual apprehension of the Divine fall into the category of proof by exclusion — for example, the Argument from Design in the physical universe (ignoring for the present the Argument from Design in the biological universe which is complicated by the contentions of the evolutionists and which therefore needs separate consideration) which has no refutation.

(Except for the possible claim that there *is no* design, that is, that the apparent plan-and-purpose and systematic arrangement of the physical universe which is such that it can be expressed in terms of inalienable laws is actually only the figment of our disorganized minds — our internal randomness interpreting the external randomness as order; this type of theorizing belongs to the category of question such as that of whether we exist at all. If one is bothered by the question of whether he is real or not and tends to favor the option of his own non-existence, one may as well stop thinking — similarly, the question of whether order is order or not has no practical expression since meaningful thought and argument have as their deepest fundamental the concept of order — namely logic; therefore in order to relate to the world at all one must accept certain premises such as that existence is real and that logic is logical. This is actually all obvious, but for one who is still troubled by the existentialist non-possibilities, a "doubt hypothesis" similar to that mentioned in relation to a practical way of dealing with the possibility of the existence of the Absolute may be helpful: since it is at least *possible* that I exist and that perceived order in the Universe is actually order and so on, I must choose to relate to the affirmative option because the negative option — I do not actually exist, etc. — is nihilistically final, it would absolutely exclude further thought and discussion. In other words, for the purpose of engaging with any subsequent issue, these fundamental philosophical issues force a decision. This should also be obvious.)

Back to the Argument from Design. Mathematically there are two ways to prove "A" — one is by derivation from first principles, and the other is by exclusion — namely, that if only "A" or "B" can be true and one can show that "B" is absurd, one has proved "A" just as surely as by derivation. The difference is that proof by derivation means that one *understands* the result — one has after all derived it from first principles and each step has been checked; however, proof by exclusion means that "A" must be true only because no alternative is possible, but what "A" *is* one does not know.

Proofs of Hashem's existence are of this sort; organization implies an Organizer; existence implies a Creation and hence a Creator since the finite universe as defined by its physical laws, which do not include the concept of creation-from-nothing and describe only conservation of matter and energy, could never have created itself (this is simply not a property of the finite). This means that we exclude the idea that the world created itself (or that it "always existed" — this similarly impossibly gives the finite a dimension of infinity!) and therefore we conclude that Something else created it, *but what the nature of that Something is* we do not know. Now when one knows something by derivation, one's understanding of it permits one to relate to it personally and immediately, but when one knows something by exclusion, one has no relationship with it other than the pure and abstract intellectual awareness that it must be so.

This is where *emunah* comes in — Hashem's existence is not in doubt, it can be proven; but since the proof is necessarily by exclusion we are left with no personal grasp of what He is or what His existence means, only a detached intellectual awareness that we are forced to accept the fact that He exists. Now this kind of knowledge *does not force one to act*; since it makes no contact with the personality, it is quite possible to know it with certainty and yet to ignore its consequences in practice — I know in an abstract theoretical sense that Hashem must exist, but since I do not "feel" this fact personally in any way, I continue to live as if He did not! *Emunah* means *living* according to the knowledge that Hashem exists, not at all the mistranslation into the concept of "faith" meaning "belief," but rather "faithfulness" (from the root נאמן meaning faithful), that is, one who has *emunah* shapes his actions and lifestyle according to that which he knows must be the truth, and his life becomes a constant affirmation of that truth; this requires the constant *avoda* of *emunah*. Knowing something and living according to that knowledge are two quite separate matters, and *emunah* represents the hard work necessary to bring them together, to overcome the tendency of the personality to seek its own gratification and ignore the voice of the intellect, no matter how immaculately logical.

METAPHOR AND REALITY

Andy was not only concerned with the intellectual proofs of the existence of the Creator, he was also concerned with our perceptions of reality. He had observed a striking inconsistency: people with enquiring minds will relate deeply to, say, a great work of literature and extract from it every subtlety of allusion, reading between the lines and beyond the literal written word, relating essentially to this level beyond all the more superficial levels as being that which reveals most significantly what the author is trying to convey. Yet they may relate to the whole Universe, of which literature itself is only a minuscule component, as if it were only surface deep and not even attempt to see the deeper harmony "between the lines."

Andy's favorite entertainment had been the cinema, and around the time that he came to the yeshiva he had seen a comedy in which the main character in a movie-within-the-movie walks off the screen into "real life." Andy had seen beyond the comedy and the question of "What is reality?" had started him thinking deeply. Much later, after months in the yeshiva, he told me a *mashal* which he felt shed light on this:

The world is like a movie; when one watches a movie he sees

---

avoda: work, effort   *mashal:* parable

only a two-dimensional illusion — a projected image on a screen. Even the origin of the illusion, the celluloid film, is itself only an illusion — the characters and events depicted on it lived in flesh and blood elsewhere in time and space. In fact if one traced those pictures back to the movie set and saw the live actors performing, far more real than the distant screen image in the cinema, even that would not represent reality — the actors themselves are only pretending to be yet other characters who may have lived in a totally different time and place or not have lived at all. Now only a fool would mistake the pictures reflected on the screen for reality; a mature understanding grasps the idea that this is only a medium and seeks to relate to the original source in order to derive the maximum enjoyment and to understand what the producer was trying to say and thereby successfully extract from the experience what was intended for him.

This world is only a dim, few-dimensioned projection of a reality which cannot be apprehended by matter-bound humans, but its beauty and glory are that all one needs to know is the very fact that it is only a medium, and one can begin to enjoy it and to learn about the levels of reality above it and which generate it, for they must be exactly parallel and analogous to it. For the poor fool who has never experienced a movie before and who would concoct every imaginable explanation for the amazing scenes which he sees, thinking that the movie is the reality (and we all do), there is an instruction manual — Torah: "Dear visitor, what you are watching is a movie. Do not confuse it with reality; you are seeing only fleeting images in a darkened room; look deeply and understand that which the eye can never see."

* * *

In yeshiva I had seen that practice often follows theory only after a definite delay; new knowledge does not necessarily mean that actions will change accordingly — an expression of the gap which *emunah* seeks to close. But knowledge does not only run ahead of action, it also runs ahead of emotions. One finds oneself knowing certain things and even being committed to the knowledge to the extent that if tested, one's actions would be appropriate, but emotionally one lags behind in the familiar ethos of one's previous lifestyle. This can lead to inconsistencies which cause distress and confusion until time produces a whole personality; and I became aware of this pitfall through my friendship with Andy. One afternoon after a few weeks of intensive learning he found me outside the *beis midrash:*

"I've had enough! I need a break. I can't take the atmosphere here right now, and I need to get out into the real world for a while. I'm going to a movie."

I had to bite my tongue not to say something about reality and unreality and all the attendant ironies, but nothing would have helped, and he needed to get out. He was suffering from acute inflammation of the gap between intellectual involvement in a new world and the deep-seated need to feel comfortable with a familiar set of values and behavior patterns. However, the movie did not help. He had chosen a movie billed as "Family Entertainment" for a couple of hours' escape, but was surprised to find that he hated every moment. The bad language, nudity (although relatively tame) and casual violence somehow jarred, and he discovered that a few months in the purity of the yeshiva environment had sensitized him. Violence shown for enjoyment? Cheapening of male-female relationships for family entertainment? I never heard him refer to the outside world as the "real" one again.

PARABLES

The next episode relating to *hashkafa* occurred shortly after this and consisted simply of a *mashal* which he heard and which gave him clarity in an area which had been causing difficulty. Having come to terms with the concept of a higher Reality and the idea that this world is only its facade, he was groping for an understanding from first principles of purpose in the world. How can we arrive at a meaningful understanding of the relationship between this world and the next and how should we understand our purpose in this one? A tape of a *shiur* by Rabbi Avigdor Miller

---

hashkafa: outlook, worldview   *shiur:* lecture

discussing a *mashal* of the Chofetz Chaim had made a great impression on him and gave him a framework for conceptualizing this issue. The *mashal* was as follows:

A man is shipwrecked. He manages to swim to an island and clambers ashore, naked and dripping. To his surprise he is greeted by a group of people who make obeisance to him and hail him as their king. They dress him in royal robes and lead him to a palace where he is enthroned, and he begins to reign. The whole situation seems strange to him but he does not confide in anyone and simply enjoys his good fortune from day to day. He enjoys royal wealth, marries and begins to raise a family. After some time however, his curiosity overcomes him and he carefully chooses a trusted counsellor, takes him into a secret chamber and asks him directly; "What is going on here?"

"It is good that you have asked," replies the counsellor, "not everyone does. I shall tell you. Every year the same thing happens, someone is washed up on our shore and is made king. He reigns over the island for a year."

"What happens at the end of the year?" asks the king.

"He is taken down to the beach, all his royal garments are removed, and he is pushed out to sea in a small boat, naked as on the day he arrived."

"Tell me, my trusted counsellor, what should I do?"

"Export," replies the counsellor. "During this year, send your wife and family and everything you own overseas and export all the wealth you can. Send everything to a secure place abroad. That is the only sensible course of action."

The king does exactly that. At every opportunity he exports whatever he can and secretly amasses a great fortune abroad.

Sure enough, at the end of the year, the courtiers and people solemnly arrive and march him down to the seashore, strip him of all his clothes, and push him out to sea, alone in a small wooden boat. But far from heartbroken, he begins rowing for the mainland — for he has somewhere to go where he is a very wealthy man.

The *mashal*, of course, is the story of life. A person is born into this world naked and finds himself dressed and cared for in royal fashion. All his needs are provided and he lives in the palace of the world. If he is wise, he looks around and asks himself: "Is all what it seems, or is there something going on here?" His trusted counsellor, the Intellect, tells him that something is indeed going on, and that it is unrealistic to pretend that life is indefinite; very soon it is all over. What should he do? Since he knows that he is inevitably bound to leave, the sensible thing to do is to export everything of value which is exportable — the non-physical commodities of Torah and *mitzvos*. The wise man spends his adult life, that phase which begins when he is able to take counsel with his intellect, engaged in spiritual growth. And when the brief year is over and he is bidden farewell and sent off in a small wooden container, naked and alone, his heart sings within him for he has family and untold wealth in a great land where existence is permanent.

* * *

Andy and I learned together in the evenings for the best part of a year. I saw him make tremendous strides in learning and his character matured almost beyond recognition. He had arrived as an unsure, tentative young man with a fractured view of the world and his place in it. He had always believed in spiritual values, commitment to friendships despite all difficulties, the importance of love and deep respect in male-female relationships and above all had an urgent need to define his goals in life; and had suffered the confusion resulting from the ridicule, both implied and explicit, of his contemporaries for being concerned with these things. His jet-set circle of acquaintances had thought him "soft" and obsessive, and he had never had a framework for defining who was right and constantly doubted himself. By the end of his stay in yeshiva he was relaxed, determined, and defining clear objectives for the kind of life he wanted. His concept of the home he wished to build centered on Torah and the deepest Jewish values of dignity and peace, and he had already laid its foundations in his own personality.

He constantly marvelled at the *hashgacha* that had helped him fight
for years to hold onto his belief in virtue and a life beyond the
here-and-now gratification philosophy of his friends and that had
finally brought him to Torah and vindication. I felt proud to know
him.

THE LAST MASHAL

A ndy left Jerusalem recently for a visit to Ohr Somayach's branch
in Monsey, New York. Our last discussion completed a cycle
of thoughts we had developed over the months. Its subject had
constituted one of the major steps in my own learning and I easily
identified with his elation as we discussed it.

By this time he was already thinking deeply about the major
issues discussed by the Kuzari and other classics, and he phrased
the following question: "Where is the evidence for the next world?
How can we see from this world that there is another?" I thought
back to his first day in the *beis midrash* and the questions he had
articulated then. This was far more sophisticated — this world
ostensibly hides the existence of the next, but since it must be an
accurate reflection of its abstract source, it must also reveal the
existence and nature of that source — but how?

I told him how the Rambam had dealt with a sharper version
of the same question. The Rambam was challenged by
representatives of a certain school of non-Jewish philosophy with
the following contemptuous attack: "Apart from a special revelation,
the only source of knowledge about any metaphysical reality is the
physical, that is, we should be able to study the physical and draw
conclusions about the metaphysical, for surely the two must be
entirely parallel."

(To postulate that the transcendent is totally unrelated to this
existence puts an end to productive enquiry because there is an
unlimited number of possible forms which that other existence
might take, and we could not be expected to extrapolate from this

hashgacha: Divine providence
Kuzari: philosophical work of Rabbi Yehuda Halevi
Rambam: Rabbi Moshe ben Maimon, Maimonides

one in order to learn about that one; and anyway, Judaism explicitly teaches that the two reflect each other exactly.)

"Now when we examine the physical universe, we see that life leads to death. This is the unvarying way of the world, and yet you Jews have the temerity to claim that there is life after death, in other words that death leads to life! Not only do you reverse what is obvious and apparent in the world, but worse, you claim to learn your inverted death-to-life process from this very world which so obviously demonstrates the opposite! Where do you stubborn Jews imagine you see clues which indicate a life after death?"

The Rambam responded essentially as follows:

Imagine a man alone on a desert island who has never seen another human being and who has no knowledge about his own origins. Imagine you arrive on his island and ask him what he supposes to be the nature of the process that brought him into existence. One can only imagine the many possible answers which he might give. Then you tell him the following: "In fact, you began life inside the body of another human being, a woman. Not only that, but you lived there for an extended period of time in conditions the very opposite of those you now experience — what is necessary for life now would have meant death then, and vice versa: you lived under water with no air to breathe. Your blood circulation was largely opposite to its present direction — blood by-passed your lungs, flowing through a ductus arteriosus, and took a strange course through a hole in your heart. Your lungs were collapsed and did not even suggest the function of gas exchange, and therefore must have seemed useless — cumbersome dead-weight, perhaps only vestigial in nature. These phenomena would spell death in your present state, and conversely, at that time an existence outside of that limited environment, the womb, would have been unthinkable — in the air of the world with no life-sustaining umbilical connection for oxygenated blood, certain death would occur almost instantly. And yet — the unthinkable happened: in a brief and critical few minutes you were ejected into that apparent death-world, and miracle after perfectly timed miracle occurred in a constellation of inversions; your previously useless lungs expanded instantaneously in time for your first breath and functioned immediately. Simultaneously your ductus arteriosus spontaneously closed, forcing blood through those lungs. Your umbilical circulation shut down with no loss of blood and in short, you exchanged one form of existence for its very opposite, an embryonic dependence on a set of seemingly unalterable life-sustaining conditions for an independent growth to sentience."

Your desert island friend would probably reply incredulously, "Do you expect me to believe that complicated tale of contradictions? My observations of myself and my world suggest no such sudden and complex conversion of a previous existence into this one."

His position may seem reasonable at first sight, it is entirely consistent with all the superficially available information, *and yet he would be wrong!*

And we, who live in a world where we do see this amazing transition, have no excuse. This is the unavoidable model for that unimaginable birth which is beyond our experience, that transition from this set of conditions, earth-bound and dark which clamor to deny any other possible form of existence, into just that: another form of existence, which is to this life as the child is to the fetus, the seeing eye to the blind.

This consummate and seminal exposition of the fulcrum of life formed our parting discussion, and it left us both with a clarity of insight into the pivotal events of our own recent lives, of *teshuva* as birth.

East To West

Jay comes from New York City. Broadly built, with dark eyes, he is a serious type who had been explicitly searching for meaning since early adolescence. After college he decided to take a trip to the "spiritual centers" of the world, mainly Tibet and the Far East, but also had Jerusalem on his list as a possibility, with yeshiva as his most extreme idea ("for something completely different"), although he had had little involvement with his Judaism since his *barmitzvah*.

He spent most of a year wandering in the East, spending up to a few weeks at each stop, trying to integrate into the lifestyle of each sect he visited in order to "feel its soul," but he failed to find one with which he felt he could identify sufficiently to warrant a deeper involvement — until he reached Thailand. The official religion in Thailand is Hinayana Buddhism and, at a particular Buddhist monastery, Jay felt something different, something that went beyond the asceticism and the dispassionate atmosphere, and he remained for some time, feeling strangely at home. On trying to identify exactly why he felt so positive he realized that the attraction lay largely in the person of the head monk who was clearly an unusual individual. He felt that the atmosphere of the whole place radiated from the presence of this man. Eventually, through subordinates, Jay requested an interview which was granted.

Two monks, in the standard simple saffron robes which left one shoulder bare, ushered him into the monastery's ornate central hall in the center of which was seated the holy man, swathed in saffron and shaven headed, with an assistant at his side.

To Jay's surprise, he was addressed in flawless English. His surprise grew when, during the course of the conversation, the Buddhist unexpectedly asked: "Are you from New York?"

"Yes," answered Jay.

"Are you Jewish?"

"Yes," he answered again, taken aback.

"Well, so am I," said the guru, and indicating his assistant, "and so is he." Then quietly, after a long pause: "I have been here for thirty years."

During the ensuing conversation Jay mentioned that he had thought of visiting a yeshiva. The guru's response to this was: "I shall give you something this evening that may help you."

That evening at the meditation session, Jay found something at his place in the meditation hall. It was an article entitled "Next Year in Jerusalem," reprinted from Rolling Stone magazine, about a young man who had profoundly changed his direction in life on becoming a student at Aish Hatorah Yeshiva in Jerusalem.

Jay left Thailand and made his way to Jerusalem. He went directly to Aish Hatorah and began learning, and later came to learn at Ohr Somayach.

When the Rosh Yeshiva heard Jay's story, he wondered aloud: "What z'chus did that far-off Yiddishe neshama have that merited him to send a young man to yeshiva?"

* * *

This story has a sequel. On his way back from Thailand Jay had travelled through India. On a particular occasion he had met two Israelis who were engaged in a search for spirituality similar to his, and they asked him for directions to the nearest center of Eastern religion. Already quite the expert, he had directed them to a local ashram.

Months later, in the dining room at Ohr Somayach, where students from the yeshiva's Israeli section eat together with the Anglo-Saxons, a heavy hand landed on his back with a thud and an incredulous voice said, "Jay?!"

It was one of the two Israelis, who had independently found his long way home.

---

z'chus: merit   Yiddishe neshama: Jewish soul

Friends

This is the story of a friendship. Five boys grew up together in Johannesburg as very close friends, and three of them now learn in Ohr Somayach. It happened like this.

Roy is a rugged-looking, sensitive type who grew up with everything. From an affluent neighborhood, he once told me that by the time he was in his early twenties he had done everything most people spend a lifetime trying to do. He had two university degrees, one in science and one in engineering, a pilot's license, had travelled overseas many times and generally had everything a young man could dream of. And yet he could not help feeling that there had to be more to life; in fact this was his prime motivation for trying yeshiva when his friend Howard suggested it. His family was Jewishly aware, his father had often called him by his Hebrew name and they had built a *succah* every year, although he had been educated at a very non-Jewish upper crust English-type school where the boys were required to attend chapel — he had had to request a special exemption. His parents were gifted with a unique insight and supported him in everything — this was to help him greatly later when he decided to become observant and learn in yeshiva.

Generally parents fall into two groups, those who become offended by and oppose their children's *teshuva*, and those who support them and often develop with them. (Occasionally in dramatic fashion. *Bachurim* at Ohr Somayach love to tell of the irate American father who had tolerated everything in his son, but

---

succah: temporary dwelling for the festival of Tabernacles
teshuva: rediscovery of Torah Judaism   *bachurim:* yeshiva students

a romance with Torah had proved too much; he had flown to Israel personally to take his son out of yeshiva for home. While they were waiting for the return flight out he attended a few *shiurim* out of curiosity. He flew back as scheduled, but alone, and it was to sell his interests and return to settle in Jerusalem and learn in the yeshiva together with his son.)

Many South African *ba'alei teshuva* have had the *bracha* of seeing their parents move towards *Yiddishkeit* with them, often prompted by the stark comparison between their *ba'al teshuva* child and his contemporaries who may have established relationships with or married non-Jews, or generally disintegrated in bad company, with drugs, or become a disappointment in some other way. The parents have identified the involvement with Torah as the source of the difference and become open to Torah themselves. Roy's parents developed a respect for what he was doing and encouraged him.

As with many of us, the Torah community in Johannesburg was instrumental in providing Roy with an exposure to Torah Judaism, and this was furthered during his engineering studies in Cape Town when he was befriended by a number of observant families who greatly impressed him. When Howard one day out of the blue declared that he was prepared to try six months in yeshiva if Roy was, Roy, although a little surprised, agreed.

* * *

Howard's family was always very closely connected with their local *shul*, one of the best known in Johannesburg, and the Rabbi had a great effect on the whole family. However, when Howard was at a younger age, on the eve of a vacation trip to Israel, the Rabbi had suggested that he try learning in a yeshiva for a while but Howard had decided to come to a kibbutz and pick fruit and was afraid of the yeshiva option and refused. He went on to obtain a degree in accountancy, and years after the kibbutz trip, an emotional and deeply thinking person, he changed his mind. He had generally matured and had shared some of Roy's experiences in the religious community, and somehow feeling that if they did

shiur(im): lecture(s)
ba'alei teshuva: those engaged in rediscovering Torah Judaism
bracha: blessing   *Yiddishkeit:* Judaism   *shul:* synagogue

not do it now they may never have the chance again, he challenged Roy to come to yeshiva with him. Neither one backed down and they came.

This was a very unusual event: for two gifted, privileged and decidedly eligible young men, in a South Africa which at that time offered unlimited opportunities, to set aside their beginning careers and enviable social lives in order to study some old books in Jerusalem for six months or possibly more demonstrated remarkable strength of character. (It also represented the beginning of a new phenomenon. Previously most of those who came to yeshiva in a planned fashion were the more unconventional types, incurable searchers of one sort or another; more recently, as the *teshuva* movement spreads, a much broader cross-section of the Jewish world is arriving; doctors, lawyers, artisans, high-school graduates, practical people who would have considered full-time Torah learning an outlandish option a few years ago now fill the *ba'al teshuva* yeshivos.)

Howard and Roy had decided to come and began preparing. The problem however, was Max. The three had been inseparable since childhood and together with the other two friends in the group had developed a unique bond of understanding. Their closeness had reached a stage where words were often unnecessary, a glance would be enough to completely share a thought or experience. They all had a tremendous, undiminishing respect for each other and an almost childlike capacity for amazement, both for each other and for the world. Howard and Roy put the proposition of yeshiva to Max; the other two had left for Australia to investigate the possibility of settling there and were not around to invite. Max was, but he refused. He had become involved in physical education and was at that time an instructor in a new method of body-building and physical fitness training which had become popular internationally, and he wanted to investigate job offers in the United States and Australia, and that was that. Although he was in a way closer to Judaism than they, having accepted many of its basic teachings from a young age spontaneously, even laying *tefillin* daily and successfully encouraging Roy to do so, he had not been in contact

---

tefillin: phylacteries

with *shiurim* on a campus or been with observant families as his two friends had, and he was simply not ready. They came to Jerusalem and he left for the States and Australia.

* * *

Howard and Roy arrived in yeshiva tentatively but almost immediately loved it. Both dived into gemara primarily and within six months became *masmidim* to a degree which startled Max when he flew in for a brief visit. That visit was a torment for Howard and Roy, however; they had been looking forward to it for weeks and had been sure that a few days in the yeshiva would convince Max, but everything seemed to go wrong. It was *bein hazmanim*, *shiurim* were sparse and many of the people whom they felt would impress Max were away. One thing did happen though, which had a powerful effect on Max and which ultimately formed one of the main factors in bringing him back to Jerusalem. The three had gone to visit Rabbi Simcha Wasserman, Howard and Roy hoping that the great man's influence would affect Max enough to challenge him into trying the learning experience. Rabbi Wasserman sized him up, taking in his fine muscular physique, and asked him in a quiet voice what he did. Max proceeded to explain his occupation as a builder of bodies and fitness.

"Fine," said Rabbi Wasserman, looking him in the eye, "and what about your mind?"

Max was speechless. "Nothing," he was thinking, but did not answer.

Howard and Roy could see the effect that this time-bomb of a comment had on him, and both flinched visibly. Months later in Australia, it was one of the factors which Max could not dismiss, and when his friends called from Jerusalem to invite him again, he accepted.

This time he came when the yeshiva was active. The *shiurim* found their mark in his heart, particularly Rabbi Aharon Feldman's *motza'ei Shabbos Mishlei shiur*. But perhaps as important was the effect of seeing his friends again and realizing how they had

---

gemara: Talmud   *masmidim:* particularly diligent students
bein hazmanim: break between semesters
Mishlei: Proverbs   *motza'ei Shabbos:* Saturday night

developed. They were tangibly greater human beings, deeper, more intense, and even more concerned about him than before. He was moved and decided to stay at least until hearing whether his immigration application to Australia had been accepted. Some months later, he heard. It was. And not only that, but a prized job had been promised to him. But he had been touched by the fire of Torah and decided to postpone it all. Howard and Roy were even more impressed with him during this phase than he had been with them; he has that unique ability to make a decision based on ideals and then follow it faithfully regardless of the difficulty in terms of life re-adjustment. He had decided to do something about his mind, and the three were back together.

One of the first things they did as a threesome was to contact the other two in Australia and beg them to visit Jerusalem and Ohr Somayach, although thus far it has not worked out. But who knows?

✳ ✳ ✳

Recently, another old friend arrived, Jody. She was a girl who years before in Johannesburg had been friendly with the five, and who had emigrated with her family to Sydney. She was now about to complete medical school there and was visiting Israel for a few weeks' vacation. She arrived at the yeshiva one day for a surprise visit, not really knowing what a yeshiva is or what her old friends were doing there. An attractive blonde, she walked into the yeshiva dressed as if she had just come off the Tel Aviv beachfront and happened to almost bump into her friends. Now a strange scene took place: Jody remembered red-blooded boys who had felt very much at ease with good-looking girls, and yet after this long separation no-one stepped forward to greet her in quite the way she would have expected. Not only that, but they were positively falling over each other in their haste to back away from her for fear that she might throw her arms around one of them, in the familiar ba'al teshuva's ever-present terror that some woman from his previous life, unaware of the religious prohibition on male-female contact even if only a handshake, will do who-knows-what to him before he can tactfully explain the situation. And not only that, but they rapidly hurried her off out of sight of the bachurim and lent her a shirt. She was amazed. So amazed that she spent Shabbos with them all at a kollel friend's home and had to hear their story, and in fact decided to visit the women's section of the yeshiva, Neve Yerushalayim, the next week.

When she said goodbye to the three of them after Shabbos she still had to remind herself that they were the same boys she remembered. She had been shaken — in her post-teenage years of maturation she had been painfully aware of how most men, beneath a thin facade, never really develop beyond their adolescent selves; in a dull way she had supposed this to be an inevitable fact of life; and here in a brief encounter with people she had known well she saw clearly that things can be very different. She went off to visit Neve that week with some radical revision of perspective.

---

kollel: advanced section of yeshiva for married students

Hidden Roots

Over the past couple of years a new phenomenon has appeared: a number of people have found their way to Ohr Somayach without knowing exactly how or why. Previously almost everyone at the yeshiva could tell of a definite chain of external events, often involving amazing *hashgacha pratis* which had brought him there, but more recently people have evolved the idea of getting in touch with authentic, Torah-from-Sinai Judaism with no identifiable stimulus. It is as if the *teshuva* movement has generated ripples which have touched certain far-flung and sensitive souls.

SIMON

Simon was brought up with no Jewish education, he had no *barmitzvah* and he could not read *aleph-bais*. On completing a music degree in Chicago he felt his lack of Jewish knowledge and identity and an inexplicable urge to find out in depth. No-one had invited him for Shabbos or to a *shiur*, in fact he had not even met anyone professing to be Orthodox, he had simply developed a personal need to know, the exact genesis of which he was never quite able to articulate.

He had some savings, Jerusalem seemed like the place to start, and somewhere or other he had heard that a place called Ohr Somayach teaches authentic Judaism in English and caters to even

---

hashgacha pratis: Divine providence at personal level
teshuva: rediscovery of Torah Judaism
aleph-bais: Hebrew alphabet   *shiur(im):* lecture(s)

the most uninformed. He went out and bought an open return ticket to Israel.

I met him as he arrived; a quiet thinker with grey eyes, all his expression was in his appearance — blond hair razor-cut short at the sides and reaching his back in the middle, multicolored plastic bangles almost to the elbows on both arms and a Mickey Mouse wristwatch. The bangles jangled when he moved. I predicted he would ask to attend *shiurim* on Kabbala and little else, but I was wrong — he began with *aleph-bais*, a course on the *siddur*, and gemara. He did everything and took everything seriously from the beginning; initially while he was learning to read Hebrew he could be seen standing *shmone esreh* long after every one else had gone for dinner.

Above all, he took to gemara. His bent had always been for the arts and he had never excelled at mathematics, but he surprised everyone with his quick grasp and clear analytical style. Soon he was in one of the relatively advanced *shiurim*, hampered only by his lack of technical skills. (This reflects the yeshiva's policy of allowing newcomers to grapple with learning at their intellectual level, providing plenty of technical help until their reading skills develop; an intellectually mature individual may be frustrated by a long introductory course in *aleph-bais*, Hebrew grammar and Aramaic before coming to grips with the challenge of gemara; this way he can start from the first day at a demanding level of intellectual involvement with gemara while he learns the basic skills simultaneously.)

After six months of hard work Simon could *daven* with the *minyan* and *"lain"* a *blatt gemara* at a basic level. His questions in gemara class were among the best, he often had a grasp of the views of some of the Rishonim on his *sugya*, and he attributed all his success to *saayta d'shmaya*. He displayed amazing evenness of character and never retreated from something he had taken on.

---

siddur: prayer book   *gemara:* Talmud
shmone esreh: lit. "eighteen"; eighteen-fold prayer central to prayer service
minyan: quorum for prayer   *daven:* pray
lain a blatt gemara: independently prepare a page of Talmud
Rishonim: Torah authorities of approx. 10th-15th centuries
sugya: conceptual unit within Talmud   *saayta d'shmaya:* the help of Heaven

He stayed for a year, and then in order to be closer to his family, went to learn in New York; he left still amazed at the unseen Hand that had brought him to Torah.

MIKE

Mike's father had learned in yeshiva in New York City until adolescence, but Mike had grown up with no knowledge of *Yiddishkeit.* Last year, just before beginning medical school at Chicago's Northwestern, Mike spent the summer doing research at Hadassah hospital in Jerusalem and decided to spend his free time at a yeshiva. He had heard of Ohr Somayach and arrived one evening for the one-hour *chavrusa* program. We were introduced and sat down in the *beis midrash* to learn, and he confided in me that he was not exactly sure what had made him decide to come, but here he was anyway and could I tell him something about Judaism.

His immediate development in the yeshiva was like a pile of tinder into which a spark has fallen; he arrived with all the common misconceptions about Torah learning and living — misunderstanding of Shabbos observance, unawareness of the existence of the Oral Law, and ignorance of any teachings concerning the mystical in Judaism. As our discussion that first evening began to explode these myths and replace them with a more mature conception of the issues, he became fascinated. One hour became many, and when we finally agreed to adjourn until the next day I had to take him to the yeshiva's library so that he could find out more by reading until we met again.

Interestingly, the rest of his course through the yeshiva summer was not all so smooth — after a few days during which he had re-scheduled his research program to enable him to spend every spare moment learning, I suddenly detected a change of heart — he seemed less sure of himself, then decided to reduce his frequency

---

Yiddishkeit: Judaism   *chavrusa:* study partner
beis midrash: study hall   *Shabbos:* the Sabbath

of attendance, and finally even cancelled an arrangement to spend Shabbos with me.

"What's bothering you, Mike?" I asked him.

"My friends," he answered. "They're telling me I'm being brainwashed."

(A very common idea among people who have never been inside a yeshiva and seen that the very opposite is true — that the environment most conducive to ruthlessly questioning and critically examining *everything* from the first premise on in an attempt to achieve true objectivity is the world of Torah.)

Soon however, he responded by inviting his friends to come and see for themselves, and their nervous refusal to set foot near the place gave him a shrewd idea of the origin of their objections — the outsider's fear of the unknown, accentuated by a decided reticence to risk beginning something which might result in a powerful challenge.

Also, like Andy, he had gone too fast, intellectually outstripping his ability to keep up in practice. He had become excited at the development of ideas, seeing the beauty of the structure of Torah *hashkafa* being built, seeing sense made of a confusing world and feeling a deep resonance of the learning within himself; but all this challenges one to act accordingly, to not only understand but to live a Torah way of life, and few can change their lifestyle overnight. A day or two later Mike decided that the solution was to study more of those areas which demand the least change of actions until he felt comfortable with them. He began to attend *seder* more, and came for Shabbos.

But that was not the end of his problems — soon afterwards he was buffeted by yet another syndrome all too familiar to new *ba'alei teshuva:*

"What will my friends and family say when I arrive with a *kippa* and refuse to eat in my parents' house?" he asked.

I said, "Mike, you've been here for two weeks. You don't wear a *kippa* now outside yeshiva or eat only kosher, so why don't you

---

hashkafa: outlook, worldview   *seder:* learning session
kippa: skullcap, yarmulke
ba'alei teshuva: those engaged in rediscovering Torah Judaism

worry about how to deal with your family and friends when keeping those *mitzvos* and *minhagim* becomes an issue?"

"But I *feel* as if I'm there already," he replied.

This is an almost universal experience among young people becoming involved in *Yiddishkeit*. Everything makes such sense and feels so much a part of the individual that he sees himself much further down the road than he actually is; and then having projected himself into the image of a perfectly *frum* Jew, often that of some particular model whom he admires, he feels a powerful dichotomy between his present self and the one he is becoming. Often the more "real" self seems to be the one he feels he will ultimately be, and a perplexing schism opens — if that is "me," how come I don't feel as if I could behave like that right now?

Mike had outreached himself in this way and it took quite some time to "catch up with himself," to feel comfortable with a vast store of new knowledge and a relatively modest progression of new observance, and to maintain a stable self-image. When this happened his initial excitement returned and he developed much more smoothly. Also what helped greatly was meeting others who had gone through the same stages and survived. The *chavrusa* program provides not only a tutor but often someone to lean on too.

Incidentally, these phenomena of losing touch with one's level can happen in waves, and a stormy course of oscillation between knowing where one is and relative confusion is standard for many *ba'alei teshuva*, again, quite the opposite of the outsider's view that "religion is a crutch" and once the "brainwashing" begins it is all a mindless production-line affair. Usually the most vociferous protagonists of this view (who are often the most fearful of trying the experience for themselves), when they do become involved are the first to appreciate the constant intellectual challenge, the uncomfortably close introspection and the agonizing over each step forward in overcoming the self; yet another example of the principle that what is thought on the "outside" is usually the direct and accurate opposite of the inside truth.

---

mitzvos: commandments   *minhagim:* customs   *frum:* observant

Mike applied for a year's deferral of his university course in order to learn in yeshiva and was refused. He considered staying on anyway and re-applying for medical school next year but was advised against doing so by the Rosh Yeshiva, advice which he accepted; and he left in time for his first semester taking with him a reading list, *shiurim* on tape, addresses of Torah centers in his area and leaving a heartfelt expression of his intention to be back next summer. His friends, of course, never understood.

* * *

While close to the source in yeshiva it is easy to be strong. The question is what happens when you leave? On your own in the jungle outside, can you hang on? I waited for news.

Last week I received a letter written in the hectic whirl of first year medical school at Northwestern. Mike spends his free time with Orthodox families in Chicago and is maintaining his learning. Also, despite difficult circumstances, he is keeping Shabbos. Mike is hanging on.

The Women

THE WOMEN

$\mathbb{W}$hen Sarah was at high school in Johannesburg she was part of a group which organized a new Jewish youth movement. They looked around for someone who could give direction and content to their meetings and somehow came across a certain Torah-observant architect whom I have mentioned before. He spoke to the group week after week, and although you might think that youth of high school age are not the most likely candidates to break with the conformity of their peers, almost all of them became observant. It is a repeatedly observed phenomenon that the spiritual "offspring" of people who are dedicated to *kiruv* become inspired to do the same, and Sarah began a long commitment to *kiruv*.

She was a brilliant student with an intense personality and also happened to be extremely talented at art, and she began a degree in fine art at university where she met Eve. Sarah's personality tends to the intellectual and philosophical, whereas Eve's is more emotionally centered, but they were both primarily concerned with the spiritual and they became friends. Both were concerned with integrity and purity and kept themselves away from the sordid side of campus life, something which was not so easy to do in those years as South Africa began its belated slide towards the permissiveness of the West. Sarah spent her free time at *shiurim* and for a long time she tried unsuccessfully to convince Eve to attend a *shiur* with her. Eve was engaged in a deep spiritual search,

kiruv: drawing people closer to Torah Judaism   *shiur(im):* lecture(s) but it never seemed to her that Judaism was the place to look; she had had a traditional Jewish upbringing and had even gone through an adolescent year of involvement with the Judaism which was available to her through the local *shul*. She had attended Friday night services and enjoyed them greatly, but no-one had ever mentioned to her that there was anything "higher," anything *spiritual* about Judaism; like most South African youngsters her impression of Judaism was one of a general morality, a group identity, family gatherings on Pesach and Rosh Hashanah, *shul* and a special meal on Friday nights, and a Zionistic love for Israel, but contained little awareness of Torah learning and no conception of the mystical element. She was part of the great tragedy of secular Jewish education, the tragedy of teaching something but not everything, for the youth not only do not know, but they are led to think they do know, and are often not interested in further investigation, sure that there can be little more to discover. Eve was essentially interested in holiness and the mystical, and she searched elsewhere.

The campus was liberally stocked with purveyors of the mystical, from Eastern sects to anthroposophy, a movement interested in the occult roots of reality. Eve was attracted by this latter group and read its material widely and deeply, attended yoga classes, and generally went along to hear any swami or guru who happened to appear on campus. Her decided aim was to become so pure spiritually that she would achieve clairvoyance, and the path *had* to be somewhere among these ostensible initiates who discussed the elevating experiences of meditation and openly claimed clairvoyance.

So for more than a year she avoided *shiurim*. During lunch hour Sarah would hurry off to hear a *shiur* on *mussar* or *halacha* and Eve would sit in a quiet corner reading a translation from Sanskrit of some work on knowledge of the higher worlds, but Sarah never gave up, and one day it paid off. She had gathered some of the Jewish girls in her art class, including Eve, on the lawn during a

---

shul: synagogue
Pesach: Passover   *Rosh Hashanah:* New Year
mussar: Torah character building   *halacha:* Torah law

break between classes, and spoke to them earnestly about the approaching days of Rosh Hashanah and Yom Kippur, impervious to their "Here goes Sarah again" resignation.

Eve was listening however, and suddenly some of the words she was hearing struck a strangely familiar note — unexpectedly she realized that Sarah was actually talking about a transcendent soul, an identity of this soul with a cosmic source, its definable structure and how the individual can become transported into realms beyond the physical; it all sounded familiar, and yet this was Judaism! Once it became apparent that there was a promise of the mystical involved, she was suddenly available for a *shiur* and the next lunch hour she went with Sarah to a talk given by none other than the same architect who had inspired Sarah years before. His disarming way of dispersing misconceptions about Judaism found its mark, and Eve hardly missed a *shiur* during her next two years on campus, leaving the "hari kiris," as students playfully referred to a certain sect, one potential member poorer.

THE TEACHERS

There were three *shiurim* a week offered on campus at that time and Eve attended them all. The second *shiur* was given by a tall, angular Sephardi Rabbi who seemed every bit as ascetic as the gurus, and yet somehow normal as well. His *shiur* opened a whole new world for Eve. His mastery of the sources was obvious, but even more impressive was his mastery of himself; watching him was a lesson in good *midos* and Eve's intuition immediately sensed his depth. She was further impressed when she became a Shabbos guest at his home — the house was relatively bare, uncarpeted wooden floorboards and simple furniture, and yet the richness of the family and the Shabbos transformed it and it was a palpable experience of elevation of the physical. The Rebbetzin was no less impressive than he was, and it was with her that Eve much later

Yom Kippur: Day of Atonement   *midos:* character traits

chose to study in preparation for her marriage. That first Shabbos in Yeoville impressed on Eve the general detachment from physicality in the Torah community; some of the homes were decidedly austere, in one she noticed there was not even a matching set of silverware, and yet she experienced an amazing feeling of contentment. The obvious focus was on people and *chesed*, and she felt drawn in and immediately at home.

The third *shiur* was by a halachic authority whose knowledge reached beyond the realm of the students' ability to measure. He would teach the works of Rabbi Dessler, the great *mussar* sage, and Eve was fascinated by the clarity of insight into the human mind and particularly by the detailed anatomy of the *neshama* which began to emerge as he spoke.

The personal qualities of these three people probably influenced their students more than what they said. The difference between them and the university lecturers was obvious — the Rabbi would remember and be concerned about a junior student whom he had met once months or even years previously, while the lecturers knew only a few of the students whom they taught daily.

Both Sarah and Eve became more and more committed to a Torah way of life and by the time they completed their university training both knew that they wanted to pursue their studies in *Yiddishkeit* further and establish homes based on Torah values. Sarah left for Neve Yerushalayim and subsequently married one of Ohr Somayach's outstanding students who has devoted himself to *kiruv* work in Jerusalem, and set up a home constantly devoted to giving others a chance to experience Torah. Eve married someone who learned in Ohr Somayach and its kollel.

TRANSITION

During the transition to Torah living, Eve became sensitized to many things. One of them was the dignity of religious women. Walking through the religious neighborhood of Geulah, in

---

chesed: kindness   *neshama:* soul   *Yiddishkeit:* Judaism
kollel: advanced section of yeshiva for married students

Jerusalem, for example, she noticed a number of things which differ from nearby Jaffa Street. The women are well dressed and modestly covered no matter how hot the weather. Men avoid looking at a woman despite her modest appearance. Married couples engage in no physical contact in public. The women radiate a self-respect and fulfillment which come from having a strong and stable family, the security of a completely faithful relationship with a husband, and the kind of community which is supportive in every way. People in general have an air of purposefulness; they are engaged in the great work of achieving something idealistic, and external political and economic factors impinge on their state of mind only peripherally. There is a pervasive sense of peace, human dignity and grace.

A few blocks away downtown however, many women, married and unmarried alike, expose themselves with no shame for anyone who cares to look. Men stare openly at whatever exposed flesh happens to be passing. Dating couples relate explicitly, unabashed. Many older faces are worried and often reflect broken lives and dreams, clearly telling of years of disappointment; attachment to the material has proved cruelly unrewarding, many families are only empty shells, women have given away their power to generate large families in the illusory hope of having more materially or for some other false ideal, they age and are left with neither, and the faces tell it all. Young faces are often vacant or full of bravado, only the very youngest do not show the painful scars of having been cheaply used, and the ambience is harsh and mercenary. Eve found the travesty of what should be an especially Jewish refinement too hard to bear; she felt that if only the women parading their nakedness so oblivious to their own indignity could see themselves for a moment with eyes attuned to genuine decency, they would understand and be ashamed. Women have become more attuned to the fickle dictates of fashion than to the timeless essential value of modesty, and Eve came to feel intimately how scrupulous attention to modesty elevates towards the uniquely human in woman.

This feeling became even sharper during her work with *ba'alei teshuva* and their families. More than once she was embarrassed at the uncomfortable summertime sight of a *ba'alas teshuva* introducing her middle-aged mother to religious friends or teachers — the mother in a frock with no sleeves, no back and not much front and imagining she looks attractive, while the daughter knows that it is only arbitrarily accepted fashion which defines such nakedness as decent, objectively, her mother is exposed and it is ugly — and yet meaningful communication between them is difficult since each lives in a separate frame of reference.

Like most *ba'alei teshuva*, during her growth in *Yiddishkeit* Eve was constantly amazed at the chasm between the misconceptions held by non-religious Jews and the truth, particularly in an area which was of particular concern to her — the role of women. The feminist movement was still popular and the almost universal concept was that Orthodox Judaism "puts women down," "in the background" or "in the kitchen," "enslaved," and generally in a very definitely inferior status. Her misconceptions concerning the position of women began to be dispelled at the same time as those concerning the supposed absence of the mystical in Judaism.

Some of her contemporaries however, did not have such a smooth adjustment. One particular American girl had been a very strong protagonist of the women's liberation movement and believed that women should express themselves in the same ways as men, and she found this idea difficult to relinquish as she grew in *Yiddishkeit*. When she finally reached the stage of being ready to study in a women's yeshiva, she arrived at Neve Yerushalayim with *tallis* and *tefillin!*

GIVERS AND TAKERS

One of the first steps for Eve was her re-understanding of dating and marriage, which began with a comparison of these processes in her former secular environment with the Torah model, but which really only became clear later as she went through these phases herself.

---

ba'al teshuva (pl. ba'alei, fem. ba'alas): one engaged in rediscovering Torah Judaism
tallis: prayer shawl   *tefillin:* phylacteries

From the very beginning the two are diametrically opposed. She had long noted a sad paradox: young women would speak in feminist terms about wanting to be seen and related to by men as a whole being, mind and body together and not simply as a "sex object," but society's norms dictate the kind of dress (and deportment) for women which result in the male's being presented primarily with the physical. The initial focus of his interest would therefore be the physical, the relationship would begin on the wrong basis and progress rapidly to include physical intimacy, often with a skew of misunderstanding if not downright deception: the girl would tend to impute to the male much more emotional involvement with her than he actually felt, his interest being more directly in the physical relationship than hers. This unhealthy relationship could be prevented only by maintaining a degree of chastity, but those girls who did were considered strange and of course, were much less popular.

However, in the Torah world the "boy meets girl" story is radically different. Firstly, the girl is modestly dressed — her body is not exposed. However, her attire is feminine — it is forbidden for women to wear men's clothing. So the male is presented not with a body but with an integrated person, attractive, feminine and with dignity. Secondly, there is no physical contact, so the relationship is predicated on the level of personality. And thirdly, since physical relations are forbidden premaritally, he has no ulterior motives and the relationship is a refined one from the beginning; the last thing in the male's mind is the woman as simply a sex object; ironically, an achievement of the feminist aim.

From the outset the relationship is serious and directed towards marriage, and the two relate to each other in the most conscious way with no crude deceptions. This element is continued in marriage — during the phase defined by the *nidda* laws when husband and wife have no physical contact, they renew and deepen this special aspect of their relationship. Of course, the same cycle also renews the physical relationship, and marriage is a cycle of constant

---

nidda laws: menstrual separation laws

re-awakening, very different from the slide into tired disappointment it so often becomes otherwise.

The sexual norms of today generate double standards — a boy will encourage and enjoy behavior in his girlfriend which he would feel very differently about in his daughters, and would personally not choose to marry someone who has conducted herself as indiscriminately as the girl he is presently dating. He has an obvious vested interest, so right now anything goes, but later when he wishes to make a more lasting commitment to a wife, he demands a far more chaste background than the one he is currently destroying in his girlfriend. The girls end up cheapened and used and usually sense it, although they repress this awareness initially because the overwhelmingly accepted norm of the present demands abandonment of virginity and reserve.

These multiple casual relationships constitute a training in how to relate superficially — what should be the single-minded devotion of a life to one other human being, a bond of unique exclusivity, is diffused into repeated and easy intimacy until the very conception of the depth of a marriage is lost. An increasingly common response is the sad decision not to marry at all; after all, in the secular system, for the male it brings only responsibility with no new privileges and limits his freedom to couple indiscriminately and indefinitely. And for those who do marry, the chances of success are relatively slim — prepared by an adolescence and young adulthood of free relationships with privilege and no obligation, the sudden change to a situation of marriage represents limitation and brings disappointment, often from the very first day. The divorce rate throughout the West and the frequent unhappiness in the as-yet undivorced speak for themselves. Eve recalled a conversation with a relative who told her of a class reunion of her day-school matriculation class seven years after graduation; of the fifteen former classmates who attended, *eight* had already been divorced, some *more than once!*

On a deeper level, Eve discovered that the key to this issue lies in the understanding of Rabbi Dessler's explanation of "givers" and "takers." Torah training generates people who are concerned with their obligations: givers. Secular values generate people who are concerned with their rights: takers. If the parties to a marriage are both givers, each seeking only to ensure the other's happiness, the result is bliss. If they are takers, the result is battle.

As her schoolfriends married, Eve saw much of this tormented reality reflected in the wedding rites of non-religious society. Before the wedding the groom attends the traditional "bachelor party," a males-only farewell to his single status. One has only to listen to the commiseration of his friends to become aware of the paradox of his situation: "There goes another good man," and "Another one bites the dust!" — a sad alcoholic farewell as if his life is about to end instead of begin, usually and significantly, more heartfelt from his already-married friends. The custom is then to display a pornographic movie, or in upper-class circles, a live exhibition of vulgarity, presumably to emphasize what the husband-to-be is about to leave behind.

And what an insult to the bride!

The wedding itself is no better. After the ceremony all the men present feel obliged to honor another important custom — to kiss the bride. Thus at the very moment of the definition of her exclusivity, everyone kisses her! And for those who argue that "a kiss is nothing," this represents a desensitization which is itself part of the tragedy.

The "honeymoon" is often the final indignity. Usually the first-night venue has to be kept secret because the groom's friends (one wonders about the term) would otherwise arrive there first and prepare any of a variety of embarrassing surprises. Much more important however, are the personal difficulties encountered by the couple. Unprepared and both somehow expecting personal fulfillment, they are often surprised to find themselves fighting and recriminating bitterly, beginning life together on a paradoxically dismal note.

Chassunas in a yeshiva or Torah community, say, in Jerusalem, are entirely different, and Eve found them exhilarating. The *chassan* and *kallah* prepare by intensively studying what is about to happen

---

chassuna(s): wedding(s) *chassan:* groom *kallah:* bride

to them; the course of study involves becoming familiar with their obligations and duties to each other and focuses on how to create a relationship of sanctity.

On the day of the *chassuna* the *chassan* and *kallah* fast, emphasizing the seriousness of the moment, and each keeps a small booklet in which friends write personal requests for *tefillos* to be said under the *chuppah*. The ceremony begins with the *chassan's* being led in a procession to his *kallah* for the *bedekking*, when he lowers the veil over her face, and goes out to await her arrival under the *chuppah*. *Tefillos* said under the *chuppah* have a special power, and the *chassan* and *kallah* spend every available moment *davening*, for others and for their own future. The whole ceremony is invested with an intense idealism, linked to the spirit of the whole Jewish people and the hope for the Redemption, and the couple fervently prepare themselves to build a home which will shine with kindness and Torah values in general.

The subsequent celebration is also striking. The guests, instead of concentrating on having a good time imbibing alcohol and dancing with other people's wives, are bound by a *mitzva* to make the *chassan* and *kallah* happy. Individuals practice special skills — juggling, balancing acts, fire-dancing, acrobatics — expressly to be able to fulfill this *mitzva* and the scene is ecstatic; perhaps more than anything else it must be experienced to be appreciated. Eve never forgot the impression she had of the first *chassuna* she attended in Jerusalem; the *chassan* and *kallah* led to the *chuppah* flanked by candle flames, accompanied by a special stirring, haunting, wordless melody, trembling in *tefilla* under the *chuppah*, and the whole hall swirling and levitating with happiness during the dancing afterwards. The experience was one of holiness and purity, and she was inspired.

During the first week of marriage there is no sudden let-down for the couple — they are feted like king and queen at *sheva brachos* — festive meals given by their family and friends. They remain together at every possible moment; in fact, for the whole of the

---

tefilla (tefillos): prayer(s)   *chuppah:* wedding canopy
bedekking: lit. "covering"   *davening:* praying
mitzva: commandment   *sheva brachos:* lit. "seven blessings"

first year of marriage extreme priority is given to this togetherness — only pressing and serious reasons permit one of them to leave the other for even a short time.

After becoming used to yeshiva *chassunas*, Eve would stand with a sense of tragedy at a non-religious wedding — she could not help seeing two people trying marriage, each jaded by previous intimate relationships with others; and statistically their marriage has more chance of failure than success. They come together under the *chuppah* with no concept of the deeper levels involved in what they are doing, no understanding of the hints, inherent in the customs of the *chuppah*, at the sublime parallels between their union and the deepest roots of the universe, aware of nothing more than the here-and-now, surrounded by equally uninformed family and guests at this greatest moment of their lives; and undreamed of and untapped, all that *kedusha* is flying past them.

CONSTRUCTION

But perhaps Eve's most significant insight came with the gradual maturing of her thinking on the essence of womanhood and its relation to home and family building. She had never accepted the current widespread attitude that a career external to the home represents fulfillment for a woman and that creating a home and raising children represent biologically forced chores which limit a woman's personal growth; on the contrary she had always sensed that to be the center of a real home was of the essence of woman, but had not been able to articulate exactly why.

In the Torah world and particularly in her own marriage she came to see a fascinating pattern emerge, beginning with the basic concepts of "male" and "female" from a Torah perspective.

Explicit in the mystical tradition, which is the source of all knowledge, is the axiom that all material reality is only a reflection of an abstract source. The ultimate Existence, which is infinite abstraction, becomes crystallized through an infinity of stages, each more concrete than the previous, until the final level which is a condensation into the physical structures and phenomena of the

---

kedusha: holiness, sanctity

world. Thus any physical entity is a concretization of an immeasurably elevated abstract. A deep enough study of the physical can therefore yield an understanding of its spiritual roots, limited only by the greatness of the investigating intellect; any observed features of the physical must be expressions, direct and faithfully accurate, of the spiritual. Man and woman therefore represent the tangible images of two supremely high Divine expressions, and a study of their biological and functional details and their interaction yields understanding of their cosmic sources.

What are the abstract roots of "male" and "female" in terms of the forces of creation?

These concepts, male and female, form the complements of any creative process. The male represents the source of the spark of inspiration; the female represents the power to accept this spark and nurture it, maintaining it alive as a generative force, into an independent entity which is itself alive and capable of further creation. The least abstracted model for this interacting duality is the biological relationship between man and woman, and the parallel is not simply an analogy, but is identical to and of the essence of the concept. The male contributes the seminal spark, microscopic in dimension and yet containing the germ of that which is to develop. The female has the ability to hold this speck of almost-nothing within herself and build it, consistently and over an extended period of time, into a complete life. She contributes its total environment, its nutrition and thus all its physical composition with the exception of the infinitesimally small contribution of the male, she is the source of maintenance of life itself for the conceptus, and the transition from dependence to independence as a complete entity, birth, is from her being.

This model operates at all levels, the male's whole expression being a constant generating of *chiddush*, creativity in its most compressed and potent form, and the female's being a mature, constant, faithful and deeply internalized giving of life to this germinal flash of inspiration. Maleness tends to the pole of infinite

chiddush: newness

conceptual genesis, femaleness to the pole of the materializing forces, the construction of reality.

In the practical world there is no pure expression of either maleness or femaleness, both men and women contain elements of each other's identity, and their relationship is therefore a complex and tightly interdependent resonance.

Eve saw that a mature understanding of this fundamental idea is the key to understanding the happiness of a Torah marriage. There is tremendous respect of each partner for the abilities of the other; each has a power far distant from the realm of the other, a man cannot nurture a pregnancy and give birth and similarly he is not emotionally and spiritually equipped for the non-physical correlates of these activities. Only a fool would argue about which set of functions is "better" or envy the other's; a wise person chooses to develop his or her particular sphere of expertise to the maximum and thrives on the complementary function of a partner in a relationship which is an organic unity.

Translated into practical terms, the consequences are obvious. While fulfillment may involve a profession, and Eve met many observant women who do express themselves in a wide variety of careers, it may just be that the greatest career is to be found in the home. An unclouded understanding of what it means to produce a child, an entire human being, is exhilarating beyond expression. Not only is the effort exerted to physically bring a life into the world, but much more difficult, to shape that new life into the greatest human being possible. This requires the constant, careful, intelligent, planned *and* intuitive molding of the home into a spiritual womb, always modelling correct behavior, self-control and devotion to higher values. It is possibly the most idealistic enterprise imaginable, daunting in its consequences which are no less than the very personalities which spring forth from that home, including those of the mother herself and her husband, quite apart from the children. The idealism, stability, maturity, selflessness and brilliant foresight required to be successful as a woman who creates such a home constitute the elements of a career which makes most others seem insignificant by comparison.

The respect due to a woman who shapes greatness in this way is beyond measure, and tragedy of the tragedies — many have been fooled by false ideologies into abandoning this potential fulfillment and go so far as to hire others to spend the necessary time with their children while they search for identity in the corporate marketplace or the political bullring, pressured by misconceptions to exchange diamonds for dust.

Part of the deception of course, has been to induce women not to have children in the first place. A correct understanding of the infinite dimensions of one human being would eliminate the idea of minimizing the number of one's children. Each child born is a gift which defies a definition of its magnitude, and the opportunity to be an indispensable part of the process of birth and subsequent nurturing to maturity with a complete achievement of potential should make a sensitive heart swell almost beyond control. While there are Torah-based factors limiting family size, the basic outlook is to maximize this amazing expression of life. The irrevocable tragedy of approaching old age and a dawning awareness that one's one-and-only lifetime was cheated of its ability to bear fruit, that one voluntarily limited what could have been many lives, many families with children of their own, generations of sparks of the Divine stretching into the future, is a pain too great to bear. It is a kind of suicide; and this willful limitation of the ability to be a channel for the Infinite is understandable only in terms of the current crude and sordid secular devaluation of human life in general.

Of course, it justifies itself by wearing the guise of its opposite — fewer children means "quality" instead of quantity, each child can be given more instead of being "deprived"; and one hears these arguments even from the wealthiest of homes, homes which could support many children royally. More "quality" means of course more material padding; the child may be given a more indulgent physical environment but is denied that priceless and irreplaceable commodity, brothers and sisters.

One has only to live in the happiness of a Torah home blessed with many children — especially when there are still younger ones around as the parents get older, and to see a mother attending her daughter's wedding and enjoying it with her youngest still in her arms — to understand.

A woman with a feeling of the holiness of children and family and their exponentially expanding eternal consequences would never sacrifice these for a short lifetime of prowess in some unrelated career for its own sake.

HIDDEN BRACHA

Eve had wondered, though, why all this must be done so modestly, so privately. Why not have a more visible, public role? Why the emphasis on *tznius*? As she learned more however, these questions were answered.

A woman's creativity is essentially internal. As much as a man's contribution to a new life demands a projection of part of himself outwards, the woman's focus is inward — she develops a child within herself entirely. The male transcends his boundaries in giving, he is *essentially* unbounded, reaching out beyond all concept of limits in spiritual terms; the female is the very definition of finite structure, she receives and holds the unlimited, she gives life itself a place to be. He is the pluripotent design, she is the finished structure.

A verse in *Tehillim* states "*Kol kvuda bas-melech pnima*" — "All the glory of a princess is inward," and the gemara says that "*ein habracha shruya ela b'davar hasamui min ha'ayin*" — "Blessing only infuses that which is hidden from the eye." This special power to concentrate her creative energy inwardly, hidden, is the basis of the exclusivity of her relationship with her husband and its entire focus. As always, this theme is the opposite of the non-Torah way, the travesty of its secular inversion in which women wear dressing-gowns and curlers at home but dress up to go out.

The more formally exposed role is the man's; in the husband-wife spiritual symbiosis he is the more apparent from the outside, he carries what is generated between them outward, while she is the

---

bracha: blessing   *tznius* modesty, privacy   *Tehillim:* Psalms

inner force which gives him a place to be. This modesty is natural to woman, and except in the most decadent societies, it is easy to see how much more women guard their modesty than men do. Understood in terms of the abstract source and its mirror-image reflection in the physical, an expression of this difference between male and female identity is genital structure — the male is built externally, the female completely internally and hidden.

TIME

Eve was still troubled by a question. Why are there different sets of *mitzvos* for men and women? Negative *mitzvos* are binding equally on men and women, including the penalties for their transgression, as are positive *mitzvos* unconnected to a time-factor. However, time-bound *mitzvos* requiring positive action are obligatory only for men. Eve had always understood this exemption of women from positive time-bound *mitzvos* to be in order to free a woman to care for a home and children — unlimited by *mitzvos* which must be performed at given times, her work as a wife and mother can be uninterrupted. But if *mitzvos* are our link with the Absolute, this explanation was inadequate. There had to be a more fundamental mechanism.

She discovered the following: this difference in *mitzvos* is connected with a difference between men and women regarding their relationship with time. Men, in a certain sense, lack a firm connection with time and are locked into it by time-bound *mitzvos*, whereas women are innately connected to time and do not need this external regulation. The reason here too springs from the understanding of the natures of man and woman — since man is the one who extends himself without limit, as it were, this central defining theme of his nature is true in all dimensions, at every point where he makes contact with the world, in the dimension of time no less than in any other. Woman however, represents the trait of concretizing reality; time, too, becomes a defined reality in her nature.

---

mitzvos: commandments

As elsewhere, it is legitimate to seek a physical expression of this spiritual difference between men and women; the physical correlate of this phenomenon is menstruation. Men do not show a physical expression of rhythmicity, whereas women show an amazing relationship with a cosmic time-cycle. The menstrual clock, often accurate to hours over a period of weeks, is difficult to link to any physical phenomenon — other biological cycles are linked to circadian triggers such as light and darkness, temperature changes, or seasonal factors such as relative day and night duration, but the physical trigger for a cycle which is constant despite external changes is hard to find; except for the moon, and it is difficult to talk about a link between menstrual timing and the phases of the moon without invoking some exquisitely sensitively tuned mechanism.

Woman has that sensitivity. Eve was aware of how greatly her understanding of herself and her world had grown. In place of a finite picture of her identity as a woman, through her connection with Torah she had reached an insight into the roots of woman and womanhood far beyond biology. She had begun to see woman as a reflection of something very high, a being tuned to the forces of creation, receptacle of Reality.

Fight for Life

If you are ever at a *chassuna* in Jerusalem, and as one of the antics that guests perform to be *mesame'ach chassan vekallah*, to fulfill the *mitzva* of causing joy to the bride and groom, you see a large, lithe figure fly through the air over six or eight crouching people and smash a heavy board in mid-air with karate kick, it is probably my friend David.

A tall, expansive character who always looks as if he is about to spring forward into some kind of action, David grew up in Baltimore where he studied criminology at college and became an outstanding black-belt karate exponent, fighting in tournaments and usually winning. His life had always been dominated by two themes — idealistic awareness of the Jewish people, his people, and a desire to fight for them in whatever way possible. In fact one of his motivations for karate training had been in order to become able to defend himself and other Jews with violence if ever insulted, and he always wore a sign on his karate suit identifying himself as Jewish; thus he felt he was always fighting as a Jew. His formal Jewish education had ceased during his childhod and its last vestige was a pair of *tefillin* from his *barmitzvah*.

After college he decided that there had to be a more Jewish expression of his burning feeling of identity, and it seemed that a move to Israel might answer this need. He came on *aliya* and

---

chassuna: wedding   *mitzva:* commandment   *tefillin:* phylacteries
aliya: lit. "going up"; immigration to Israel

studied at an *ulpan*. But driven by a nature that is always seeking the ultimate challenge, the same feeling soon took hold of him again — just living in Israel did not seem to fulfill his constant desire to be fighting for his people, and after six months in *ulpan* he volunteered for the Israeli Army's paratroop corps, perhaps the toughest branch of the service. The dangers held no fear for him; on the contrary, it seemed to him that to die with a gun in his hand, asserting and defending Judaism, would be worth everything.

He was accepted, underwent the torture of paratrooper training and felt it was all worthwhile when he was awarded his red beret at a ceremony in the shadow of the Western Wall after an all-night, eighty kilometer forced march carrying a man on a stretcher and with no rest. Later he earned his wings with the small proportion of men who completed the course.

But still he was not satisfied. It seemed that there had to be more. Risking his life in defense of Israel and his brothers somehow did not fulfill his desire to be constantly expressing the flame of Judaism, and one Yom Kippur in the army something moved him to put on a *kippa*. He decided to become religious since that would be a permanent and intrinsic identification with the eternal aspect of Judaism, although he had no idea of what was involved. He would be wearing his *kippa* and would find himself knowing less than some of his non-religious friends, and soon decided that he had to learn how to be a Jew.

As the date of his discharge from the army approached he considered the idea of going to Ohr Somayach for formal instruction in the *mitzvos*, but was apprehensive — he wanted to know more and yet felt the prospect to be daunting; there seemed so much to have to know, and he was essentially a man of action. He was also secretly hesitant to take on the obligation of all *mitzvos* at once, and felt that if he became involved even slightly in structured learning he would immediately be committing himself to a vast unknown system with unforseeable consequences. In fact, he strongly desired an attachment to the deepest level of *Yiddishkeit*

ulpan: Hebrew study program
Yom Kippur: Day of Atonement   *kippa:* skullcap, yarmulke
Yiddishkeit: Judaism

and found himself in the dilemma of many would-be *ba'alei teshuva* in the stage before taking the plunge. On one occasion he saw a group of young men on the street who were offering passers-by the opportunity to don *tefillin*. He desperately wanted to put on the *tefillin* and be reminded of the details of the *mitzva*, but his fear kept him at a distance. After a while he walked by quickly, so that they should not have time to accost him, and yet illogically hoping they would.

The day after his army discharge he went to Eilat for a vacation with the idea of having a few days' peace in which to make a decision: yeshiva, or take up a job which he had been offered as a karate instructor to the Israeli police. He arrived in Eilat and went to the soldiers' home, a hostel for soldiers on post-service vacation, and was given a room to share with one other person. As he entered the room, to his surprise he found a tall, bearded man — his roommate, who turned out not only to be religious but working at Ohr Somayach at the time. That was enough for David. The next day, his intended vacation entirely forgotten, he returned to Jerusalem and presented himself at the yeshiva.

He stayed for three and a half years. He had come expecting a course in practical observance of the *mitzvos* and discovered a whole world. He soon began to feel a deep sense of home — here was that rich depth he had been sure must exist, here he felt immersed in his Jewish people, not only in the present but eternally, stretching back millennia and still going, a nation whose identity was far more than much of modern day Israel with its cheap copy of Western culture; a nation of fighters in the deepest sense, like himself; a people who had fought to the death for much more than mere survival again and again, amazing heroes who had carried the battle both externally to Canaanite, Philistine, Greek and Roman legions, and far more difficult, into the inner recesses of the self. He was moved to tears as he came to know the true face of his people and came to understand the meaning of his blind drive to fight for them. He began to feel excruciatingly that each one was his brother or sister, from Rabbi Akiva being tortured to death by

---

ba'alei teshuva: those engaged in rediscovering Torah Judaism

Roman legionnaires, his flesh raked off his bones with iron combs and yet enraptured at the opportunity to say *Shema Yisrael* with his last breath, to the young mother herded by leering German soldiers towards her death with a newborn baby boy in her arms, who asked the German officer for his knife as a last request, which he happily granted — her suicide would be entertaining — and instead who knelt on the ground over her baby, recited the blessing and performed his circumcision as her last act on earth.

He was angry at his own lack of knowledge and misinformation about distant Jewish history and wept bitterly with trembling indignation at his shameful miseducation about recent events — he had always heard that six million Jews gave their lives like lambs, passive nondescripts who deserve the indulgent sympathy of modern Jewish warriors, and discovered the opposite, that those butchered saints had withstood carefully planned torture intended to dehumanize them, to show the world that the Jew is an animal like anyone else, and had fought with each other to *give away* their last scrap of bread, had given their shoes away when called out for execution so that warm shoes should not be wasted but be used by another living Jew, had refused to bribe agents for a prized passport for a child because some other unknown Jew's child would die as a result, had fasted on Yom Kippur although assured of torture if they did; and quite incidentally, when they *had* been able to fight physically had done so with a fierceness which had caused the whole organized, mechanized and well-fed German army heavy losses. He spoke to people who had been there and heard about how Jewish girls had fought for their modesty no less bravely than the legendary young woman during a medieval German pogrom who was dragged through the streets by her hair behind a horse — as she was being tied to the horse she borrowed long hairpins from an old lady bystander and pinned her skirts to the flesh of her thighs so that she should not be exposed during her ordeal.

These insights moved him to a rage at the modern distortion of values. Scripture and gemara both explicitly and kabbalistically associate beauty with the effort to remain far from immorality;

Shema Yisrael: declaration of G-d's unity   *gemara:* Talmud

today's world associates beauty with indulgence in the immoral. Jewish girls had died for their virtue; in modern-day Baltimore and Tel Aviv they are giving it away free. Those had scrupulously covered their bodies and these are advertising all. Like all *ba'alei teshuva*, he began to understand a major key to growth in Torah *hashkafa*, that the truth is the opposite of its immediately available superficial version, and that whatever one's secular grasp of an issue, the spiritual concept will be the opposite. Not only are the Jewish people physically in *galus*, on a deeper level truth is in *galus*, and if one learns something in today's ambience without much searching and effort, it is probably wrong. The *geula* will be more than geographical, it will be the most fundamental revision of values imaginable.

*   *   *

David gradually worked through all the basics, unlearning and re-learning, constantly opening new dimensions in his Jewish identity and pride.

Like many *ba'alei teshuva*, particularly in Israel, he came to the point where he could not understand how he had ever thought differently, and in fact began to wonder how irreligious Israelis identify at all since the current concepts are so diametrically opposed to those of genuine *Yiddishkeit*, but an interesting experience reminded him that the deepest root of Jewish feeling is not dependent on correct intellectual understanding only. It happened during the war in Lebanon. After some time in yeshiva he was called into action and during the fighting he discovered a deep-rooted and very Jewish feeling in many of his fellow soldiers — on one occasion he was putting on his *tefillin* by the roadside deep inside enemy territory, those same *tefillin* which he had kept from the time of his *barmitzvah*. Soldiers around him whose units were mobilizing to move on and who had no time to put on his *tefillin* themselves, ran over and clutched onto the straps, shouted *"Shema Yisrael!"*, some of them for the first time since their youth, and ran on into battle. He wondered how much the charged emotions of the battlefield were responsible but later became aware

---

hashkafa: outlook, worldview   *galus:* Diaspora   *geula:* the Redemption

of similar scenes involving Israelis not under pressure — one of his friends in the yeshiva had been an educational officer in the army and had come to yeshiva because he realized he knew nothing about Judaism although his task was to educate and motivate others about it, and he told the following story:

He and a friend had been on the train to Haifa on a particular occasion when they found themselves surrounded by dozens of undisciplined Israeli high school students — loud, aggressive and looking for trouble. It was time to don *tefillin* and the two of them began to do so. One or two of the youngsters in the carriage jeeringly asked what they were doing, most had never seen *tefillin* before. They quietly explained something about *tefillin* and their spiritual significance, hardly expecting to be heard, much less understood. Suddenly the carriage grew quiet, and after a pause, two of the boys approached and asked if they could try to put on the *tefillin*. They did. The rest of the trip to Haifa was taken up by all the boys on the train coming over in two's and three's and donning *tefillin*, seriously and with awe. Experiences and tales like these mellowed David and he was able to immerse himself in his studies with a mixed and semi-healed picture of his secular environment.

One other awareness during the Lebanon campaign also left its mark and contributed to his *emunah*. He had always thought that Israelis win wars because they are good, well-organized fighters, but in Lebanon he saw Hashem's hand clearly, firstly in his own deliverance from great danger on more than one occasion, and secondly when he realized that these soldiers functioning correctly, these tank drivers obeying orders to drive into the fire with no regard for their own safety, are in civilian life the taxi drivers of Tel Aviv who will not take orders from anyone, will not cooperate on the road or in fact obey any rules at all. Here one might assume that they would think of lots of convincing Israeli arguments about why they should retreat instead of advance, and yet they do not. They advance; they become heroes. On Dizengoff they may be used to hustling for themselves, here they risk their lives to save others.

emunah: faith   *Hashem:* lit. "the Name"; G-d

Forty days later, he came out of Lebanon and returned to yeshiva. He married a girl whose father had been with the Mir Yeshiva in Shanghai during the Second World War, and settled in Jerusalem. Today he learns in one of the best kollels and feels, strangely, that he is only now really beginning to fight; fighting with the few against the many to recapture the real spirit of Israel, to re-awaken the love of Jews for Hashem despite the derision of the majority, fighting to lift them from an abyss of agnostic dissolution to unity as the people of Hashem.

* * *

His prime motivation in life had been his love for his people, and it remained so. But in yeshiva he began to search for an intellectual understanding of the "specialness" of the Jewish people — why should there be a "chosen" people in the first place? Emotional and quick to act, he had never stopped to work out the rational aspect of this question and now he felt the need to do so. As with so many other issues, the *mashal* was provided by Rabbi Wasserman. Once a week Rabbi Wasserman would visit the yeshiva for a question-and-answer session devoted to beginners, and on one occasion he illustrated the subject along the following lines:

In any large-scale business operation there are various departments, such as advertising, maintenance, manufacturing and so on. But the one which justifies all the others is the sales department. In fact, if the business is profitable all other departments may actually cost money to run, as long as the sales department delivers the goods and makes a profit for the organization as a whole. Now the Universe is Hashem's business investment. There is therefore human endeavor in the world which generates no profit in spiritual terms but provides maintenance only, as it were; vast sections of mankind may be involved in upkeep of the physical world and its social infrastructure, but if the whole of humanity were purely self-maintaining and produced no output other than its own perpetuation, where would be the achievement of purpose? (Of course, the same question is valid on an individual level too: a person

---

mashal: parable   *kollel:* advanced section of yeshiva for married students

who works in order to eat in order to continue working in order to eat and so on, as so many people tragically do, is devoting the prodigious capabilities inherent in a human existence to no more than maintenance, ignoring his potential for producing that which goes far beyond mere survival and which is actually the purpose of his existence.)

On the universal level, there must be a segment of humanity which shows a profit, which generates from the physical infrastructure that which rises above it and justifies it. The Torah nation is given that opportunity — Torah is the very definition of purpose, the ultimate profit, and if the world is brought to its moral and spiritual perfection by the force of Torah learning and practice, all is justified.

In explaining the role of Torah as the absolute *tachlis*, Rav Wasserman, quoting the Rambam, gave a striking illustration. Just as when a *rebbe* gives a young *cheder* boy honey as he learns in order to induce in him a love for learning, Hashem provides us with reward for Torah; no less than the infinite sweetness of *olam haba*. But the amazing thing is that the motivations of the giver and the taker are opposite: the *cheder* boy learns because he wants honey, while the *rebbe* gives honey because he wants learning to result. And if one can grasp the cosmic implications, it is the same with Hashem and us — we live and learn Torah in order to merit a share in eternity, but Hashem, as it were, gives us a share in that eternity because He wants Torah!

* * *

When I last saw David he was trying to re-organize his day to squeeze in a few more minutes of learning. He is still fighting. And winning. Behind that flying side-kick is a hero.

---

tachlis: purpose   *rebbe:* rabbi, teacher
cheder: religious elementary school   *olam haba:* the world to come

Aliya

R ael is from a small town in the Transvaal. As is the case in most South African Jewish families, he grew up with a strong sense of Jewish identity but no Torah learning apart from some elementary instruction during his junior school years. Gifted with brilliance and a particularly single-minded intensity, he distinguished himself in two ways: one was that he came to Johannesburg to study medicine and maintained a record as the best student in one of the best classes that the University of the Witwatersrand medical school ever produced, winning the top internship posts in both medicine and surgery and earning an extra science degree on the way with published research in human physiology.

The other is that he became the leader of a major South African Jewish youth movement. What this movement is requires some explanation. It is a national movement involving a large segment of Jewish youth; in some of the smaller centers a majority of the youth are members. Many of our parents were members in their day. It has a secular Zionist ideology and its highest ideal is to come on *aliya* and settle on a kibbutz, usually as part of a group known as a *garin* or "seed" group. However, even for those who never come to Israel it provided perhaps the major part of its members'

aliya: lit. "going up"; immigration to Israel

Jewish education, developing awareness of Israel — the land and its history, Jews in other countries, Jewish history and so on. Perhaps its most important contribution however, was in the area of challenging young people to think — social systems, interpersonal relationships and many other subjects formed the themes of meetings and seminars, and creative debate abounded. *Madrichim* carefully planned meetings which were the highlight of the week for thousands of us. The atmosphere was richly idealistic and for many of the movement's senior members it was the central issue and focus of their lives. Many graduates of the movement are aware that they received more "education" in a creative sense during their years of participation in it than they did at school.

The highlight of the movement year was the summer camp at the seaside in the Cape. Over a thousand children and teenagers would spend three weeks under the guidance of *madrichim* usually no older than eighteen or nineteen, and it was an unforgettable experience, including hikes in the mountains of the stunningly beautiful Cape Peninsula, sleeping in tents or under the stars around a campfire, and a high level of intellectual discussion. Organized activities extended into the night and included crafts, scouting, folkdancing, singing and learning Hebrew. At those camps a new *garin* was often formed, its members committing themselves to come on *aliya* in the near future. Lifetime friendships began and a sense of maturity and responsibility was developed in the *madrichim*. The final responsibility for this enterprise rests with the *Mazkir Klali* (General Secretary) of the movement who is the *Rosh Machaneh* (Head of the camp), and it was while Rael held this position during his medical student years that he began to detect a change in the movement which made him begin to re-assess his involvement. What had become apparent was a gradual shift in values which was undermining the movement's idealistic base.

What had happened was the following: the movement had never had an immutable nature — being non-religious it was subject to a re-definition of its tenets and goals by each generation of its leadership, and it was the personal quality of its leaders which set

madrichim: guides, leaders

its standards. In our parents' generation and until recently the integrity and moral standards maintained were high, due probably to most Jewish South Africans' relative closeness to a Torah-imbued generation (most adult South Africans have parents or grandparents who came from Lithuania) and the conservative nature of South African society.

But then the values of modern society began to make inroads. When Rael was a ten year old in the movement, for example, strict discipline was maintained, members wore uniforms, wrote tests and earned badges of rank; smoking was prohibited and at the year-end camp boy-girl relationships were relatively reserved or at least discreet, but by the time he was *Mazkir Klali* there was almost no formal structure and no uniform; at camps discipline was a problem and male-female relationships had lost all semblance of reserve. At the last camp Rael attended he witnessed the unbelievable irony of Jewish girls of fifteen and sixteen sent by their parents for a "safe" holiday in a Jewish environment only to become involved with one or another of the three Portuguese Angolan mercenaries who were paid to provide security for the camp. Some of the older girls were involved with the lifesavers, non-Jews from Durban; in fact a lifesaver boy-friend was a status symbol.

At the same time on an ideological level the movement had begun to fail; earlier generations of *garinim* had left home, lived together in a commune-style *bayit* (home) with socialistic sharing of funds, those working supporting those still at university until the time came for *aliya*. The individuals who led the movement and came on *aliya* were its best sons and daughters — mostly intellectuals, university graduates who had studied political science, sociology, arts or social work, with a disproportionately large number of medical graduates. They came to Israel and kibbutz, many remained and can be found today on a number of kibbutzim around the country. But in more recent years the pattern had changed drastically — the level of commitment was much lower, and of Rael's contemporaries who came on *aliya* few are left in Israel let alone on kibbutz; they found that simply living in Israel in an agriculturally based lifestyle did not constitute a total fulfillment of their personalities and today they may be found in California, Chicago, Boston, or back in South Africa.

This disillusioning process, part of the general and rapid shift of values among South African Jewish youth, formed part of the motivation for Rael's re-assessing his future as a secular Zionist. Incidentally, this downhill slide of values and morality is in general completely unbelievable to South African Jewish parents — they grew up in such a stable, ethical and decent ethos that they cannot imagine the low-level status quo now existing among their children; their teenage years were spent in honorable fashion, dating was a relatively chaste affair, dating non-Jews unusual and intermarriage scandalous. They often react to their children's becoming *ba'alei teshuva* with "Why do you need all this religiousness — we turned out decent without it!" not realizing that firstly, they *did* have it in the form of a deeply rooted and very Jewish transmission from their parents, and received in a far more ethical and chaste age, and therefore, secondly, that the chances of today's Jewish teenager "turning out decent," that is, preserving virginity, avoiding intermarriage, able to maintain *any* marriage for more than a few years or even months, and to be motivated to provide a Jewish education for *his* children are decidedly slim. This split of values is graphically illustrated by a number of families which have been shattered by a child's marrying a non-Jew and the parents reacting by severing relations with the child in a total non-acceptance of the intermarriage; yet in many of these cases the child received absolutely no Jewish education. How could parents provide no education against intermarriage and then react so strongly to the inevitable result? The explanation again, is that in the context of the *parents'* upbringing it was quite clear that Jews married Jews and they simply took for granted that their children would understand and adhere to such a value, projecting their own deep-seated Jewish identity and healthy xenophobia onto their children; but the present generation of youth who have not lived through a holocaust or experienced vicious anti-semitism and in addition have been taught no defenses are ready to intermarry in frightening proportions.

* * *

---

ba'alei teshuva: those engaged in rediscovering Torah Judaism

Rael's feeling that the movement had begun to move away from its ideals made him ready for a major paradigm shift. Unlike his thinking American counterpart who searches for meaning in a vacuum of existential anxiety and finds Torah as a result, Rael began a search for personal integrity.

The final break with secular values came during a student elective which he spent in the United States. He worked in neurology and pediatrics at two of the best hospitals in New York and Boston and experienced American medical training at its technical best and human worst, interns and residents unashamedly jostling to bump each other off the academic pyramid. Among American youth in general the apathy of the 'seventies was stalking, there was a depersonalized amorality and a mood of inarticulate desperation. He stayed in Greenwich Village, which did not help at all. With a South African student friend he went to see a movie about marriage in which each character ended up having a sexual relationship with most of the others, homosexual as well as heterosexual, and instead of being a satire it was supposed to be a comedy. The two of them sat uncomfortably while the rest of the audience laughed. When he received a letter from his fiancee saying that she had been going to *shiurim*, he made an easy decision — he would return to South Africa and start learning.

The decision and its implementation filled him with relief. He had always tended towards authentic Judaism, but the right framework had never presented itself. Years before, on a junior leadership course in Israel, he had spontaneously bought a pair of *tefillin* and begun using them. Later, again in Israel on *machon*, the course of preparation for senior leaders of the movement, he had felt inexplicably drawn to the Orthodox Jews he met; once, on a Jerusalem street with some friends, he was struck by the glow of purity and happiness of some Chassidic children and pointed them out to his friends: *"That's* the way to be!" he had said suddenly and emphatically.

"Are you crazy?" they turned on him. "We're universalists, remember?"

---

shiurim: lectures   *tefillin:* phylacteries

His naive, small-town morality had never accepted the permissiveness of his contemporaries; but now instead of feeling awkward and old-fashioned, he began to see that his view was in fact the closer to genuine human dignity.

On his return he began learning in one of Johannesburg's *kiruv*-oriented Torah communities. The expressed open-mindedness of the youth movement did not extend to Torah, and it soon became apparent that the only option was to phase himself out. Once the brief transition was complete however, he was faced with a new problem — being an all-or-nothing personality, he plunged headlong into *Yiddishkeit* and as many *ba'alei teshuva* discover, the initial involvement in Torah can bring pain as well as pleasure. He found much of his past surfacing with emotion which was often difficult to control, a period of cathartic cleansing. For a few months he was unable to *daven shacharis* with a *minyan* because when he began to *daven* tears would pour from him. Once his sister-in-law walked into his apartment while he was *davening* and he had to cover his face with his *tallis* and leave the room. Often the Shabbos atmosphere of peace and harmony would paradoxically draw unexplained tears, its potential for elevation matched by an equal and opposite quality depending only on the state of the receptive heart for its expression.

Gradually the phase of pouring out the old passed and the roller-coaster emotions settled into *simcha*. Rael subsequently met these stages of growth in others; in him they had been more pronounced though, because unlike many who step across the divide with one foot while keeping the other planted in the world of their former lives for security before the final move, his nature had demanded a clean and complete jump. *"L'fum tza'ara agra"* — "According to the difficulty, so is the reward."

When the emotional dust cleared, Rael found himself in an amazing world. During the heightened sensitivity of those first months of grappling with the learning, two main perceptions

---

kiruv: drawing people closer to Torah Judaism
Yiddishkeit: Judaism   *daven:* pray
shacharis: morning prayer service   *minyan:* quorum for prayer
tallis: prayer shawl   *Shabbos:* the Sabbath   *simcha:* joy

crystallized in his consciousness. One was the obvious happiness and sense of fulfillment of the personalities involved in Torah learning, particularly those who have achieved a degree of mastery. Early one morning he was sitting in the Kollel library in Urania Street when an English Chassidic Rabbi who has learned in the Kollel for years, alone in a corner or in a quiet room above the *beis midrash* and become unique in the process, entered. He was looking for a *sefer* and as he rapidly scanned the shelves singing his Torah song, intent and totally absorbed, Rael suddenly perceived his aura of *simcha* and elevation. He was clearly in another world, transported by his learning, and even in the simple act of looking for a *sefer* it was easily apparent. Rael was inspired.

The other was the consistency with which things started to fit together. Previously he had seen the world as consisting of various separate realities which often conflicted, and now, the more Torah he absorbed, the more all things showed themselves to be facets of a single theme, a great unity. Few insights generate a happiness as deep as this.

At around that time Rabbi Mendel Weinbach visited South Africa; his *shiurim* left a deep impression on Rael and caused him to think seriously about Ohr Somayach. Rael's love for Israel had never diminished and soon after marrying, he and his wife decided to come on *aliya*. They settled in a Torah community, Rael working as the community doctor at night and learning at Ohr Somayach by day, and doing both with his customary intensity. Despite the simultaneous responsibility of caring for patients he rapidly advanced to kollel level. His day begins before dawn with the sunrise *minyan* and ends with the last patient late at night.

* * *

The two themes of his former life were medicine and the youth movement. That he did not choose a career devoted purely to medicine has left him with no regrets. But his movement life and his separation from it have left him with one regret: his friends.

Friendships in the movement were special and one does not forget

---

kollel: see glossary   *beis midrash:* study hall   *sefer:* book

them. All *ba'alei teshuva* know that the hardest people to interest in what they have done are family, especially parents and older brothers and sisters; they remember you when you were without knowledge, *they* always taught *you*, they changed your diapers; that makes it very hard for them to receive enlightenment from you now. Friends are easier. But movement relationships were so tightly enmeshed that it was more like a family, and when someone has changed so significantly as Rael had, a reaction of involuntary polarization is set up immediately. So of all his acquaintances the ones most difficult to speak to, to be given a true idea of what he has found, are those with whom he was closest, and yet they remain the most important.

And there is a deeper reason for the difficulty. The secularist believes that he is completely open-minded and that the man of faith is completely narrow; in his secular frame of reference he is willing to consider all possibilities, while his view of his religious antithesis is that he must remain within the confines of a totally rigid system. However, the ironic and tragic truth is just the opposite. Faith means being faithful to the search for truth no matter where it leads; the man of faith is prepared to continually move beyond his present conception of reality, to transcend himself, his perceptions and his world, to transcend the very limits of possibility, to travel *no matter where the road may lead.* He is an Avraham, following an intimation of truth to an unspecified land, leaving completely and permanently all that he calls home for a goal which could be absolutely anything, with no preconditions, with total sacrifice of every last vestige of connection with familiarity. When the path leads from one paradigm to a greater, more inclusive one, he must be prepared to sacrifice the former before he can enter the new; if he seeks to apprehend the greater reality from within the prism of the lesser, it *must* shrink and distort to fit that prism; the honest seeker must utterly destroy his entire frame of reference even before he knows what the alternative will be. *That* is faith. And it is broad beyond all notion of limitation; its very definition is that which always goes beyond present limits.

The secular thinker however, is exactly the opposite. He is

prepared to move anywhere — *as long as it is within the known limits of existence*. His colossal precondition is that there can be nothing beyond the universe of his definitions, the universe of human experience, and consequently right from the start, the end can be predicted: his road will never, *can never* lead beyond the edge of his own perceptions, the limits of his own being. There is nothing narrower than this, and its bitter irony is that as long as he stands within it, he can never see it. His total universe is no more than the starting point of the man of faith.

The movement held that *aliya* is the ultimate achievement. Rael agrees. But *aliya* means more than a geographical change to him, it is a "going up" in the deepest sense, a journey to a very high land, and that journey is constant. Rael is on his way and he misses only the company of his friends on the road.

Heart and Mind

For a long time I had an evening *chavrusa* with Steve. Particularly good looking, with dark hair and very blue eyes, square jaw and irresistible personal *chein*, he was very quiet about himself and his background and I discovered his story only after knowing him for quite a while. He had grown up on the East Coast of the United States, at college had obtained a degree in industrial psychology and worked in personnel management. The unusual part of his history began when, on a visit to California, he became involved in a quasi-Eastern sect of the kind which seems to be indigenous to California. His personality is extremely mature and stable, he is the kind of person who analyzes the possible consequences of a decision before acting and would seem the least likely candidate for becoming attached to any fringe element, and one can only wonder at the force of attraction the sect and its leader must have exerted in order to have sucked him out of his seemingly complete and fulfilled lifestyle. However, he was searching at the time, asking the great questions concerning ultimate purpose in life that young adults often ask in the phase after the scramble of obtaining an education ends and settled adult life is about to begin. For many, this is the "last chance" to re-assess the direction of their lives before committing themselves to long-term responsibilities and it is during this phase that certain courageous and idealistic individuals occasionally make radical changes of direction in an attempt to escape the prospect of a life of unalleviated normality.

chavrusa: study partner; here: learning session with a partner
chein: charm emanating from within

The sect centered around the personality of its self-styled leader. An American whose background was strikingly ordinary, he claimed to have had a "revelation" and achieved "nirvana" during his college years, and attracted a group of followers unusually dedicated to him personally and to his ideas. The sect's ideology was an adaptation of Buddhism, and its practice laid heavy emphasis on meditation and an attempt to "merge with the universe" in a grand depersonalization. Later, in yeshiva, Steve showed me a publication of the sect. It was a highly professional glossy paperback produced by the sect's own publishing house, consisting of the writings of the leader ("I am the Buddha. I am the Universe.") detailing his growth to "consciousness," and high-quality photographs of this man during meditation — an unusual, childlike and strangely charismatic-looking character, in various yoga poses and surrounded by lilies and incense. It seemed that the group's attraction was mainly for intellectuals, its rarefied ideals of self-negation and universalism drawing an intelligent cross-section of college graduates and California truth-seekers, predictably, many of them Jewish. Steve's life became intimately involved with them and he spent three years as a practitioner in the sect.

So what brought him to *Yiddishkeit* and yeshiva?

Over the years, he had a close friend, Jeremy, who had spent six months at Ohr Somayach and never stopped trying to persuade him to try the learning experience for himself. Steve had never felt it to be necessary however, and eventually they ended up at opposite ends of the continent, Steve in California and Jeremy in New York. Jeremy would call regularly and repeat his requests, but Steve was completely involved with the sect and never agreed.

After three years of this unchanged situation Steve received yet another call.

"Steve, this is Jeremy. I know you're not interested in going to yeshiva, but how about if the yeshiva comes to you?"

"What do you mean?"

"There's a three-day seminar run by Ohr Somayach in California this weekend. Would you consider going?"

Yiddishkeit: Judaism

"Well, I don't know," hesitated Steve.

"Three days," said Jeremy. "That's all. What can you lose? After three years in that . . ." Words failed him for a moment, and then: "Do it for me, Steve. Surely our friendship is worth three days?"

Steve agreed to go. Not that he expected to discover anything, though. He was only doing it for his friend.

The Ohr Somayach team presented a dynamic course with *shiurim* on Torah *hashkafa*, and the seminar included an intense Shabbos experience, but Steve was largely unimpressed. He had arguments for everything and parried every issue, discussing many topics with the yeshiva men until late at night, defending his chosen lifestyle and ideology.

Until the very last *shiur* at the end of the third day.

It was a talk by Rabbi Gottlieb; Steve remembers it clearly, and probably always will. The sparkle-eyed Bostoner *chassid* teaches one of the most popular courses in the yeshiva, and many a new student is amazed to learn that he was Professor of Analytical Philosophy at Johns Hopkins before coming to Ohr Somayach. But it was not the subject of the *shiur* which affected Steve, it was something Rav Gottlieb mentioned in passing. He was speaking about education and the purity and special quality of children in Torah homes, and happened to mention that his own young daughter regularly gave a considerable share of her very small allowance to *tzedaka*. Steve noticed with surprise that the Rav had tears in his eyes as he spoke. Suddenly, as if a heavy veil were being lifted, he had a glimpse into the warmth of a Torah home, the transmission of selfless values from parents to children, the deep understanding between parents and children, and in a moment he was flooded with an awareness of the contrast between a real home with living Torah values and his own sterile situation.

Always the logical thinker, he had been reached on a level beyond logic.

After the talk he spoke with Rav Gottlieb for a long, long time, and soon after, he arrived in Jerusalem. At around the same time members of the sect initiated litigation against their leader charging

shiur(im): lecture(s)   hashkafa: outlook, worldview
Shabbos: the Sabbath   tzedaka: charity

him with extortion and misappropriation of funds.

Steve's arrival in yeshiva was, in Rabbi Avigdor Miller's words, a case of "boy meets gemara." He proved to be exceptionally talented at learning and rose through the *shiurim*. I recall many occasions when, although still hampered by a relative lack of technical skills, he cut through to the heart of a *sugya* before I did despite my several years' head start in learning. After a couple of years in Ohr Somayach he moved to the yeshiva's Zichron Yaacov branch, and I still miss his inspiring presence in the *beis midrash*.

✳ ✳ ✳

As is the case with any of us, Steve's growth in understanding and the development of his former ideas to a Torah conception would alone fill a book, but perhaps one particular theme stands out. Much of his mental energy while involved with the sect had been devoted to working on rising above the physical. He had perceived asceticism to be central to any form of spiritual growth and had studied it in the context of non-Jewish religions in general.

Non-Jewish conceptions of spirituality have as their ideal total separation from the physical — their highest exponents are ascetics and celibates subsisting on minimal diets in remote environments with little company and forbidden many aspects of the material, as if to reach elevation one must first deny and transcend the earthly. In Judaism he noticed what seemed to be the opposite — the path of Jewish spirituality involves a relationship with and elevation of the physical; food, marriage, in fact all aspects of life, perhaps ideally illustrated by the use of wine — while the non-Jewish concept is that alcohol is either a focus of excessive indulgence, and in fact presents a formidable ordeal to much of the non-Jewish world, or else must be avoided entirely, the Jew uses alcohol specifically at occasions of spiritual significance, *bris milah* and the marriage ceremony, as well as for *kiddush*, the very name meaning "sanctity."

But this understanding led to confusion: in the classical *mussar*

---

gemara: Talmud   *sugya:* conceptual unit within Talmud
beis midrash: study hall   *bris milah:* circumcision
kiddush: Sabbath and festival sanctification over wine
mussar: Torah character-building

works he found the theme of *prishus,* meaning "separation" or abstinence from the physical, and its centrality in Jewish spirituality expounded. So what was the Jewish ideal of *prishus?* Where is the "separation" from the physical if our highest saints marry, drink wine and use the material world fully?

The answer was provided by Rabbi Wasserman in a discussion on the meaning of "right" and "left." Why are right and left associated in many languages with "correct" and "wrong"? What is "sinister," or "wrong," about the left?

Rabbi Wasserman explained that the function of the left is to help the right, it is auxiliary and dominated by the right, and as long as the right dominates and the left assists, the left achieves its purpose and fulfillment. Imagine however, if the left took over and attempted to dominate. Unskilled for primary functioning, chaos would result. The perfection of function of the left lies in its very subservience.

So it is with the spiritual and the physical. The spiritual should dominate and the physical assist. If the physical aids the spiritual purpose and is only a vehicle for it, it in itself achieves holiness, it is a function of spirituality and is thus elevated. If however the physical becomes an end in itself, it becomes ugly and far worse than neutral.

The spiritual purpose of eating, for example, is to sustain the body for its *tachlis* of serving Hashem. The physical aspects of food include its appearance, taste, smell and the enjoyment it provides. Now the correct approach to eating should be as follows: a human being seeking to become elevated should eat with the prime intention of fortifying and sustaining the body in order to continue serving Hashem, and the physical adjuncts of appearance, taste, smell and the general pleasure which the food provides should be harnessed to this central intention. If this is done the two aspects, dominant and secondary, come together and both are sanctified.

If however, the physical is allowed to dominate, that is the individual, although say, not at all hungry, decides to indulge in food purely and exclusively for the pleasurable sensation of its taste,

---

tachlis: purpose   *Hashem:* lit. "the Name", G-d

he becomes lower than animal, involved entirely in physicality for its own sake. Therefore the concept of *prishus* is to "separate" oneself from involvement in this world *for its own sake;* however, far from rejecting the world, one uses every detail of it as an adjunct to the spiritual purpose, and in the process achieves holiness of the self and the world itself. The strange paradox which results however, is that the physical, when used in this way, yields *more* pleasure than when used as a simple indulgence because it becomes linked to the unlimited dimension in man which is where real pleasure lies.

Also, there is a higher element involved in a Jew's use of the material, such as on Shabbos and Yom Tov, when the tension between physical and spiritual worlds disappears and it becomes a *mitzva* to enjoy the physical *itself,* dominant and auxiliary, right and left, merging on the plane of *tachlis.*

This explained a lot for Steve. He had never been able to conceive of the whole beautiful material world as no more than a *nisayon,* or test, created only to be rejected by man. It had always seemed to him that it must have a positive purpose too, a use which in itself could result in achievement in spiritual terms, and he now had a glimpse of understanding into how this is true and how all aspects of the Creation are true in the deepest sense. Since becoming involved in *Yiddishkeit* he had seen many novices caught in the difficult ordeal of trying to achieve *prishus,* imagining that it means denying themselves all physical pleasure, even trying to avoid tasting food while eating it. Now the beauty of the world took on a deeper significance, and Steve understood on a new level the subtle task of relating to that beauty while engaged in the *avoda* of *prishus,* that uniquely Jewish element in the path to greatness.

Yom Tov: the festivals   *mitzva:* commandment   *avoda:* work, effort

Lighthouse

Some people develop gradually in *Yiddishkeit*, each stage of growth merging imperceptibly with the next, while others can look back and define the quantum jumps which brought them to the present. Ari is of the latter group. A South African, he studied literature and the development of Western thought before deciding to come to Ohr Somayach.

In the large *beis midrash* one lunch hour, golden Jerusalem light streaming in through the high windows, I asked him to trace the development of his thinking over the past four years at the yeshiva and kollel. We had come of age in this place, as it were, and it seemed to me as if the *beis midrash* itself was listening to our conversation.

Much of his growth of consciousness related to a particular theme — the idea of man as an unlimited creation. Shortly after beginning to learn he had heard that the name אדם "*adam*" (man) is composed of the same letters as the word מאד "*me'od*" — which means "very" or "very much." Hebrew letters and therefore words are not simply arbitrary denotations accepted by consensus, but rather, constitute the essence of the object or concept which they describe (rooted in the idea that the world was created by Hashem's saying the words and thereby creating the objects which at their deepest level are those words themselves; the very word for a "word" and an "object" is the same: דבר "*davar*"). It therefore follows that of the essence of man's existence is that aspect of his being which is always "very," that which reaches beyond the self in a continual cosmic extension

Yiddishkeit: Judaism   *beis midrash:* study hall
Hashem: lit. "the Name"; G-d

beyond quantification. One pole of his being is rooted in אדמה "adama" (dust), but the other is a boundless transcendence, as opposed to animal existence which is denoted by בהמה "behemah" (animal) which at root expresses the idea that the essence of its being is "within it," circumscribed by the borders of its physical existence.

In the secular world man is seen as having no higher dimension at all, he is simply a biological organism in an ecosystem; in fact, animal. The tendency to see man in this light, to limit him to the immediately apparent dimensions, explains many diverse and seemingly paradoxical observations; Ari had often noted that objects of idolatrous worship in various cultures are human in form, ranging from primitive totems to religions in which some or other human, whether conceived of as prophet or superhuman in some way, is worshiped. He began to understand that when man is the center of his own universe, even when he is moved to look beyond himself for a model or a focus of adulation, he finds only a projection of himself. Torah teaches that man is an image of Hashem; idolatry makes a god of an image of man. With such a limited model of reality one's universe can never be greater than the self, and one's own limitations are projected to form the boundaries of existence. The individual and his society are mortal and mutable, therefore his morals change continually. As he drifts through changing circumstances his moral frame of reference mutates to accommodate him and does not prescribe imperatives but simply describes his behavior after the fact.

Even logic and rationality are not indispensable. Ari had been deeply upset by a popular book he had read while becoming involved in *Yiddishkeit* — the subject was the classic question of suffering: why do good people often suffer and bad people often not? It was unashamedly written by an apparently Jewish author and claimed to arrive at its conclusion via an analysis of Scripture. Its unbelievable thesis was that the Absolute Being who created the universe from nothing is not quite powerful enough to see that justice is done. He can manage everything else, from the Creation itself to the giving of the Torah, but is not absolute when it comes to reward and punishment. In other words the Absolute is not absolute. This idiocy deserves no analysis and he would have ignored it as a minor embarrassment to Judaism, except that it rapidly became a bestseller. Ari was at a loss to understand such a phenomenon. The incomprehensible proposition that the Divine, which is the definition of infinity in every possible sense, should have a limitation, and moreover that this limitation should be specifically in the area of morality, the very reason for the Creation in the first place, defies rational thought; but what makes masses of ostensibly literate people accept such inanity? It had bothered Ari for a long time, and now he felt the glimmer of an understanding. If man is at the center and is himself the creator of his own conceptual universe, then the universe will look like him; and if he injects the concept of a deity into that universe, the deity will also look like him. Since he himself is limited, of course, his god will be too. To say nothing of his logic.

This also explained the tortured involvement with the question of suffering itself. In the secular world, since the universe and everything in it are seen as proportional to the magnitude of the human intellect, anything beyond human understanding cannot exist. If justice is postulated to exist and yet good people suffer and vice versa, and the individual cannot see the account ultimately balanced, he is at a painful impasse. Ari heard from Rabbi Wasserman how his father, the great Reb Elchonon, had illustrated a Torah perspective on this issue in the ghetto before his martyrdom. Reb Elchonon was replying to a question about the inferno of suffering in the ghetto and among European Jewry in general at that time, and gave the following *mashal:*

"A man who has no idea about agriculture visits a farmer. He is surprised to see the farmer cut deep furrows into the earth. 'You are ruining a beautiful field!' he objects. The farmer behind his plough answers patiently, 'Wait and see why I am doing this.' Later, he is horrified when bags of grain are strewn over the ploughed ground — 'Why are you wasting good grain?' Then he is puzzled to see water poured out on the ground. He imagines he has a glimmer

mashal: parable

of understanding when green shoots appear above ground, but when the wheat is fully grown he is again surprised to see it cut down, and even more so when it is crushed to powder in a mill. Then half of the resulting material is thrown to the wind! The farmer bears all his outbursts with patience. When he sees the fine flour mixed with water to form a thick paste, he is again perplexed, but his amazement is extreme when the lumps of dough are placed in a scorching oven. 'You'll destroy them!' he cries.

"Now if this obtuse individual would leave at that or any previous point in time, he would remain perpetually puzzled. Only if he is present to see the fresh loaves of bread emerge from the oven will he understand the long process he has witnessed.

"So too, we see only a part of the picture. Only one who sees the whole chain of events, from the beginning to the very end, can hope to understand."

Since man is finite but his context is not, he can never see and understand the whole. The wise man knows this, but the fool demands that reality fit into the ambit of his vision; he does not see a world-to-come, so he seeks a balance in this world; he does not even see all of this world, and yet has the arrogance to demand equity in that fragment of it which he experiences.

✳ ✳ ✳

This line of thought explained something else too. Ari had come across a gemara which states *"Gadol hametsuveh ve'oseh mimi she'eyno metsuveh ve'oseh"* — "He who does because he is commanded is greater than he who does without being commanded." He had found this difficult to understand — surely one who acts spontaneously is greater than one who is forced by a *mitzva*? After all, he generates the action in and of himself, whereas the one who responds to an imperative is directed by an external motivation; surely the former is greater?

The answer had come from his gemara Rebbe: When a person

---

gemara: Talmud   *mitzva:* commandment   *rebbe:* rabbi, teacher

does something spontaneously, unmotivated by any external factor, he is expressing himself. Now, just as in logic one can never go beyond one's premises, so too here, the individual can never express more than what he is; no matter how personally accomplished, at best his action will be an expression of his totality. However, when one acts because of a Divine command, he is locking into an unlimited dimension; the source of the action is in the infinite, and there is no limit to the height that can be attained. Once again, Ari saw that the true measure of the human being is the transcendent element and that the mistaken conception is that which sees the human as contained within his own immediate boundaries.

✳ ✳ ✳

On a societal level the same principle seemed to operate. Society sees itself as all-encompassing and manufactures values appropriately. This was brought home to Ari with graphic clarity during a *shiur* given by Rabbi Yaacov Weinberg of Baltimore's Ner Israel Yeshiva on a visit to Aish Hatorah in Jerusalem, and it formed one more of the clear landmarks in his growth which he could pinpoint.

Rabbi Weinberg was discussing certain values central to the Western cultural ethos and showing how they are actually meaningless fabrications. Ari was amazed to hear the list include "Adventure," "Etiquette," "Romance," "Fair play" and "Chivalry." Rabbi Weinberg pointed out that these concepts do not even have names in Hebrew, a sure clue that they do not exist in reality. But most of the audience had trouble accepting this idea — what is wrong with "fair play" (as opposed to "fairness," or justice; "fair play" being the specific chivalry of "not hitting a man when he is down," ensuring that the parties to a duel are equally armed, that hunter and hunted are on equal terms, and so on)? Since most of the students were Americans, Rabbi Weinberg illustrated the idea of "fair play" by considering, of all things for a Rosh Yeshiva, that particularly American genre of movie, the Western.

"Picture a typical Western," Rabbi Weinberg had said. "First

---

shiur: lecture   *Rosh Yeshiva:* head of yeshiva

comes the villain, black as the Ace of Spades. He rides into town and begins butchering men, women and children. In due course the hero arrives, dressed in white and wearing a silver star. The two face each other in the main street in single combat; shutters are down, the dusty street is deserted and faces peer out from behind the shades. Silence, as each man's gun-hand hovers motionless over his holster, and then: 'Draw!'

"At this point, one must analyze what is happening. Because we know that in this stylized morality play the forces of good will certainly triumph over the forces of evil, we accept the scene. But a healthy morality should ask in horror: What do you mean 'Draw'? If the hero is faster, that's good for the men, women and children, but if the villain is faster, too bad for the men, women and children! Now what justification is there for gunning a man down in the street? Surely only to save those men, women and children, and therefore, if it must be done, *shoot him in the back!* Under no circumstances can there be a justification for giving the villain a 'fair chance'; the lives of men, women and children are at stake; they depend on his execution, and the correctly trained moral mind would cry out for the hero to execute the villain in the most immediate and sure way possible. Giving him a 'fighting chance' means that the game must be played at all costs, in fact the game is everything, and the notion of 'fair play' comes before the lives of those who must be saved!"

Ari was stunned. Until then he would have given a lot for "fair play," perhaps even have risked his own safety without thinking. This central value in today's morality had just been exploded. And Rabbi Weinberg went on to dismantle the others: "Adventure? What *meshugenner* goes out to face death simply for the sake of the experience itself? Surely only someone who has such a lack of a sense of being alive that he must face death for the adrenalin shot that it gives him in order to feel alive. Coming close to death gives him a temporary sense of life, and he is to be pitied, for he lives only from one dangerous 'shot' to the next. A fulfilled individual does not have to risk his life in order to experience it,

---

meshugenner: madman

life is continually exciting for him without artificial 'fixes'."

And so on, taking apart much of what the unthinking accept as noble and necessary. If the values are generated by human agency they will inevitably be human in their fallibility.

That memorable *shiur* signalled one of the most significant points in Ari's reconstruction of his frame of reference. Above all it made him think critically, and he resolved never to take anything for granted in the future.

✳   ✳   ✳

Later, at a juncture when he had to make certain practical decisions about his future, he heard a *shmuess* by a *mashgiach* which helped him greatly and defined another memorable step ahead. A *mashgiach* must be able to pin down subtle issues and peel away the layers of human self-interest to reveal clarity, and so it was on this occasion.

Paradoxically, the subject concerned an area in which it is the secular misconception that strives for minimizing limitation whereas the Torah ideal encourages the individual to define boundaries in a particular sense. The subject was that of human potential. The *mashgiach* explained that youth is the time of greatest potential and the natural tendency is to attempt to maintain potential in its most open form; for example, a yeshiva *bachur* may hesitate to marry because while a bachelor he has the exhilaration of the awareness that he can marry any one of a vast number of potential partners, whereas when he actually marries he will be limited to just one wife! This limiting of potential is interpreted as a loss, but of course the fallacy is that while the potential exists for almost any woman to become his wife, *as yet he has none*, whereas when he marries he acquires a real asset in exchange for the price of relinquished potential. The immature mind seeks to maintain all possibilities, the mature individual is ready to exchange his currency of potentialities for real achievement. The work in *mussar* terms is firstly, to define one's particular circle of capabilities accurately and to divest oneself simultaneously of the desire to be great in all areas outside of that

---

shmuess: discourse   *mashgiach:* spiritual supervisor in a yeshiva
bachur: yeshiva student   *mussar:* Torah character-building

circle; and secondly, to set about becoming as great as possible in one's defined and chosen areas.

This results, among other things, in the absence of jealousy, because the individual alone can maximize his particular constellation of talents, no-one else in the world has exactly the same set; and he has no cause to envy anyone else's given lot since by definition he could not possibly achieve greatness in any but his own. Youth should be spent getting to know one's abilities acutely and intensively, and adult life spent refining and building the personality in those areas which have become apparent as maximally promising; a successful old person is one who has given away all his potential for maximum acquisition, he is rich in spiritual and personal terms. Ari knew that the Hebrew word for an old person זקן comprises זה קנה meaning "he has acquired."

The tragedy of the opposite view is that one can reach old age having juggled all possibilities "successfully" and not have achieved anything in practical terms. The *mashgiach* illustrated this with a story:

A Russian peasant farmer found himself, due to circumstances, with no land to farm. As he stood weeping the Czar happened to pass by in his carriage and stopped at the sight of the unhappy man. When he heard the tragic story of the farmer with no farm he was moved to rectify matters: "I shall give you all the land you desire," he said, and driving a stake into the ground where they stood, he gave the farmer three similar stakes and instructed him to walk in one direction as far as he wished, then plant a second stake in the ground, turn right and repeat the procedure — after walking once again as far as he wanted, to plant the third stake, turn right and walk until he decided to plant the fourth, and all the land between the four stakes would be his, a gift from the Czar — the size of which was entirely up to the farmer to determine. The man thanked the Czar for this wonderful gift, took the three stakes and began walking.

After a good distance he was about to drive a stake into the earth and turn, when he thought: "Why should I turn here? I could walk a little further and have a larger property," and continued; and as the story goes, he never stopped walking.

* * *

In the transition to become a *ben-Torah* the whole being is involved, the emotions no less than the intellect, and pain is inevitable. As his worldview changed, Ari found himself agonizing over those of his family and friends who had remained behind, as well as for all of the Jewish people who have not yet discovered their link with eternity. The *ben-Torah* sees this world as an access to the next and uses it accordingly; the secularist who believes that there is only this world expends himself in a futile attempt to devour it all. Ari was struck by a description of this phenomenon which he heard from a great Rosh Yeshiva in Jerusalem:

This world is like an egg; if you handle it carefully it will hatch into a reality as alive as an egg is inanimate. If your shortsighted focus is on instant gratification and you do not understand this concept, you take your egg and eat it. Foresight and a little patience with an egg and you would have had a chicken, that chicken would have produced more eggs, those eggs would have become more chickens, and you would have had more eggs and chickens than you could imagine, without end; but you settled for an omelette.

And since almost all of today's world lives in that way, what is happening is the spiritual equivalent of cities of people consuming themselves alive, tearing the flesh off their bones and gulping it down until they no longer exist. A little patience, a little thought, and they would guard and nurture that priceless human essence to its fulfillment as the seed of eternity.

At root it is the pain of this awareness and the consciousness that their world is our world that motivates yeshivos like Ohr Somayach and *kiruv* efforts everywhere. Ari had spoken through

---

ben-Torah: one whose life is entirely consistent with Torah
kiruv: drawing people closer to Torah Judaism

most of the lunch hour, and as he fell silent we both became aware of the atmosphere in the quiet *beis midrash.*

A few *masmidim* were engrossed in their books, oblivious to the time of day. Near the *bima* the *mashgiach*, Reb Naftoli, was listening intently to the fervent emotion of a *talmid.* Towards the back a new student had entered when everyone else had left for lunch, and struggling with the *brachos*, had put on a new pair of *tefillin.* A long shaft of afternoon sunlight bathed him as he stood, eyes closed and motionless, for as long as we had spoken. I think we both had the same feeling at that moment; a vision of the transition of lives and the knowledge that this place is, in a deep way, the fulcrum of the world.

---

masmidim: particularly diligent students
bima: platform in synagogue used for Torah reading
talmid: student   brachos: blessings   *tefillin:* phylacteries

Glossary of Hebrew and Yiddish Words

aleph-bais: Hebrew alphabet

aliya: lit. "going up"; immigration to Israel

aveiros: transgressions

avoda: work, effort

Avraham Avinu: our forefather Abraham

avreichim: kollel students

ba'al teshuva (fem. ba'alas, pl. ba'alei): one engaged in rediscovering Torah Judaism

bachur(im): yeshiva student(s)

bedekking (Yiddish): lit. "covering," bridegroom's lowering of bride's veil before wedding ceremony

bein hashmashos: twilight

bein hazmanim: break between semesters

beis midrash: study hall

ben-Torah: one whose life is entirely consistent with Torah

bima: platform in synagogue used for Torah reading

blatt gemara (blatt — Yiddish): page of Talmud

bracha (brachos): blessing(s)

bris milah: circumcision

challa (challos): Sabbath bread

chassan: bridegroom

chassuna: wedding

chavrusa: study partner

Chazon Ish: Rabbi Avraham Yeshaia Karelitz, of Lithuania and later Bnei Brak

cheder: religious elementary school

chein: charm emanating from within

chesed: kindness

chiddush: newness, new thought

Chofetz Chaim: Rabbi Yisrael Meir Hacohen Kagan of Radin

chozer beteshuva: current Israeli usage for *ba'al teshuva*

chumash: the Five Books of Moses

chuppa: wedding canopy

chutzpah: cheek

daf: page (of Talmud)

daven: pray

divrei Torah: words of Torah

emunah: faith

erev Shabbos: day before the Sabbath

frum (Yiddish): observant

gadol, gedolei Torah: man or men great in Torah

galus: the Diaspora

gehinnom: dimension of retribution in the hereafter

gemara: Talmud

geula: the Redemption

hachnasas orchim: hospitality

halacha: Torah law

Hashem: lit. "the Name"; G-d

hashgacha: Divine providence

hashgacha pratis: Divine providence at personal level

hashkafa: outlook, worldview

kallah: bride

kedusha: holiness, sanctity

kehilla: community

kiddush: Sabbath and festival sanctification over wine

kippa: skullcap, yarmulke

kiruv: drawing people closer to Torah Judaism

kollel: (1) advanced section of yeshiva for married students; (2) [cap.] a *kehilla* in Johannesburg

Kuzari: philosophical work of Rabbi Yehuda Halevi

lain a blatt gemara (Yiddish): independently prepare a page of Talmud

madrichim: guides, leaders

masechta: tractate of Talmud

mashal: parable

mashgiach: spiritual supervisor in a yeshiva

masmidim: particularly diligent students

mensch (Yiddish): lit. "person"; colloq. decent human being

meshugenner (Yiddish): madman

Michtav Me-Eliyahu: classic *mussar* work by Rabbi E. E. Dessler

midos: character traits

minhagim: customs

min hashamayim: from Heaven

minyan: quorum for prayer

mishkan: the Sanctuary

Mishlei: Proverbs

mitzva (mitzvos): commandment(s)

motza'ei Shabbos: Saturday night

mussar: Torah teaching on character development

neshama: soul

nidda laws: menstrual separation laws

olam haba: the world to come

perek: chapter

Pesach: Passover

peyos: sidelocks

posek: halachic authority

Rambam: Rabbi Moshe ben Maimon, Maimonides

Rashi: famous 11th century Torah commentator

Rav: rabbi

rebbe: rabbi, teacher

Rishon(im): Torah authorities of approx. 10th-15th centuries

Rosh Yeshiva: head of a yeshiva

saayta d'shmaya (Aramaic): the help of Heaven

seder: learning session

sedra: weekly Torah portion

sefer: book

sevaros: logical constructs

Shabbos: the Sabbath

shacharis: morning prayer service

Shema Yisrael: declaration of G-d's unity

sheva brachos: lit. "seven blessings"; said at wedding ceremony and during subsequent week

shiur(im): lecture(s)

shiur klali: comprehensive lecture

shmone esreh: lit. "eighteen"; eighteen-fold prayer central to prayer service

shmuess (Yiddish): discourse

shul(s) (Yiddish): synagogue(s)

siddur: prayer book

simcha: joy

succah: temporary dwelling for the festival of Tabernacles

succah shel livyasan: succah made of the skin of leviathan

Succos: festival of Tabernacles

sugya: conceptual unit within Talmud

ta'avah: lit. "desire"; involvement in the physical

tachlis: purpose

tallis: prayer shawl

talmid: student

tefillin: phylacteries

tefillos: prayers

Tehillim: Psalms

teshuva: rediscovery of Torah Judaism

Torah shebe'al peh: the Oral Law

Tosefos: group of medieval Talmudic commentators

tzaddik: righteous individual

tzedaka: charity

tzitzis: fringes hung on four-cornered garment

tznius: modesty, privacy

ulpan: Hebrew study program

yetzer hara: negative inclination

Yiddishe neshama: Jewish soul

Yiddishkeit: Judaism

Yom Kippur: Day of Atonement

Yom Tov: festival

z'chus: merit

zman: semester

zmiros: Sabbath table songs